fun & funky knitting

fun & funky knitting

30 PROJECTS FOR AN EXCITING NEW LOOK

Emma King

Martingale
& COMPANY

Martingale
& C O M P A N Y

Martingale & Company
20205 144th Avenue NE
Woodinville, WA 98072-8478 USA
www.martingale-pub.com

Reproduction by Anorax
Printed and bound by Kyodo, Singapore
10 09 08 07 06   9 8 7 6 5 4 3 2 1

Library of Congress Cataloging-in-Publication data is
available upon request.

ISBN 1-56477-684-0

Mission Statement
Dedicated to providing quality products and service
to inspire creativity.

Commissioned and edited by Marie Clayton
Project managed by Carly Madden
Designed by Ben Cracknell Studios and Gemma Wilson
Photographed by Sue Baker and Michael Wicks
Pattern checked by Marilyn Wilson

contents

introduction

Knitted accessories are fun to make and give you a chance to experiment with colors
and yarns to create eye-catching designs. This collection of accessories, my second book, includes hats,
scarves, bags, and even some jewelery, meaning you will never be without a little knitted something
to brighten up your wardrobe!

Projects range from big chunky bags and belts to delicate knits using fine yarns, beads, and even wire.
While working through these projects you will have the chance to try out techniques and learn new
skills such as knitting with beads, stitch work and color work.

Color is the inspiration behind all my designs. There are so many wonderful yarns and shades available
that I am never without a new combination or idea to try out! I hope that by following the patterns in
this book and working with my palette and yarn choices, you will also try out some yarn and color
combinations of your own. In some of my designs I have used finishing touches such
as knitted flowers, frills, and twisted cords for extra fun! All these are quick, simple additions that can
embellish many projects or outfits so why not make a "Petal Corsage" for every day of the week. One
in pinks, one in greens, one in purples…the possibilities are endless!

I hope you have fun knitting these designs and find inspiration to keep on knitting and accessorizing!

emma king

yarns and materials

Choosing the right yarn

If you want your accessories to look like the pictures in the book, I would recommend that you use the yarns that I have specified for each design. A substitute yarn that differs in weight, shade, or fiber content will change the whole look, feel, and size of the finished project.

Quantities and dye lots

At the beginning of each project the quantities of yarn are given for the bag. If different yarns are used, these quantities will alter. This is because the length of a ball of yarn depends on its weight and fiber content: an aran-weight cotton will have a shorter length than an aran-weight wool, and a 4-ply cotton will have a longer length than a double-knit cotton. The quantities of yarn can be recalculated if desired. Buy all the yarn you need to complete the project at the same time, checking the ball bands to ensure that all the balls are from the same dye lot. The color of a specific shade of yarn can vary quite a lot between dye lots and the change will show in the finished project.

Yarn used in this book

A selection of yarns from the Rowan Yarn collection have been used to knit all of the designs in this book. Following is a guide to the yarns used.

II Seasons Cotton
Aran-weight cotton and microfiber yarn
60% cotton/40% microfiber
Approximately 98 yd (90 m) per $1^3/_4$ oz (50 g) ball

Big Wool
Super chunky pure wool
100% merino wool
Approximately 87 yd (80 m) per $3^1/_2$ oz (100 g) ball

Calmer
Soft cotton mix
75% cotton/25% acrylic/microfiber
Approximately 175 yd (160 m) per $1^3/_4$ oz (50 g) ball

Chunky Print
Chunky pure wool
100% wool
Approximately 109 yd (100 m) per $3^1/_2$ oz (100 g) ball

Cotton Glacé
Lightweight cotton yarn
100% cotton
Approximately 125 yd (115 m) per $1^3/_4$ oz (50 g) ball

Felted Tweed
Lightweight double knitting
50% merino wool/25% alpaca/25% viscose
Approximately 191 yd (175 m) per $1^{3}/_{4}$ oz
(50 g) ball

Handknit DK Cotton
Medium-weight cotton yarn
100% cotton
Approximately 92 yd (85 m) per $1^{3}/_{4}$ oz (50 g) ball

Kid Classic
Aran weight mohair mix
70% lambswool/26% kid mohair/4% nylon
Approximately 153 yd (140 m) per $1^{3}/_{4}$ oz
(50 g) ball

Kid Silk Haze
Very lightweight mohair yarn
70% super kid mohair/30% silk
Approximately 230 yd (210 m) per 1 oz (25 g) ball

Lurex Shimmer
Very lightweight lurex yarn
80% viscose/20% polyester
Approximately 104 yd (95 m) per 1oz (25 g) ball

Plaid
Chunky wool blend
42% merino wool/30% acrylic fibre/28% superfine
alpaca
Approximately 109 yd (100 m) per $3^{1}/_{2}$ oz
(100 g) ball

Ribbon Twist
Super Chunky
70% wool/25% acrylic/5% polyamide
Approximately 66 yd (60 m) per $3^{1}/_{2}$ oz (100 g) ball

Rowan Denim
Medium-weight cotton yarn
100% cotton
Approximately 101 yd (93 m) per $1^{3}/_{4}$ oz (50 g) ball

Summer Tweed
Aran-weight silk and cotton yarn
70% silk/30% cotton
Approximately 118 yd (108 m) per $1^{3}/_{4}$ oz
(50 g) hank

Wool Cotton
Double-knitting wool and cotton
50% merino wool/50% cotton
Approximately 123 yd (113 m) per $1^{3}/_{4}$ oz
(50 g) ball

Yorkshire Tweed 4 ply
4 ply pure wool
100% pure new wool
Approximately 120 yd (110 m) per 1 oz (25 g) ball

Yorkshire Tweed DK
Double knitting pure wool
100% pure new wool
Approximately 123 yd (113 m) per $1^{3}/_{4}$ oz
(50 g) ball

4 ply Soft
Fine pure wool
100% merino wool
Approximately 191 yd (175 m) per $1^{3}/_{4}$ oz
(50 g) ball

4 ply Cotton
4 ply pure cotton
100% Cotton
Approximately 186 yd (170 m) per $1^{3}/_{4}$ oz
(50 g) ball

working from a pattern

Before starting any pattern, always read it through. This will give you an idea of how the design is structured and the techniques that are involved. Each pattern includes the following elements.

Materials

This section gives a list of materials required, including the amount of yarn, sizes of needles and any buttons or zippers. The yarn amounts specified are based on average requirements and are therefore approximate.

Abbreviations

Knitting instructions are normally given in an abbreviated form which saves valuable space. In this book the most commonly used abbreviations are listed on page 9 and additional abbreviations specific to a project are listed on the project page.

Project instructions

Before starting to knit, read the instructions carefully to understand the abbreviations used, how the design is structured, and in which order each piece is worked. However, there may be some parts of the pattern that only become clear when you are knitting them, so do not assume that you are being slow or that the pattern is wrong.

Asterisks or brackets are used to indicate the repetition of a sequence of stitches. For example: *K3, P1; rep from * to end. This means, knit three stitches, then purl one stitch, then repeat this sequence to the end of the row. It could also be written: [K3, P1] to end. Asterisks and brackets may be used together in a row. For example: *K4, P1, [K1, P1] 3 times; rep from * to end. The part

of the instruction in brackets indicates that these stitches only are to be repeated three times before returning to the instructions immediately after the asterisk.

When repeating anything, make sure that you are doing so the correct number of times. For example: [K1, P1] twice means that 4 stitches are worked, but *K1, P1; rep from * twice more means 6 stitches are worked.

The phrase "work even" means continue without increasing or decreasing the number of stitches and keeping the established pattern correct.

When you put your knitting aside, always mark where you are on the pattern; it is better to be safe than sorry, especially if a complex stitch is involved.

If the numeral 0 appears within an instruction, for example, "K1(0,1,2) sts." this means that for that particular size no stitches are worked at that point. Take special care if the sizes have been separated for a particular instruction. For example, suppose that the pattern states "1st and 4th sizes only Cast off 15 (20) sts, work to end." For the 1st size, follow the instructions outside the round brackets, and for the 4th size follow those within them. For any other size, these instructions do not apply.

Finishing

The Finishing section in each project will tell you how to join the knitted pieces together. Always follow the recommended sequence.

Gauge (tension) and selecting correct needle size

The needle sizes that I have recommended for each design have been chosen to create a firm gauge (tension). This is especially important if you are knitting accessories that are going to be handled, such as bags. If the knitting is too loose, the article will easily become misshapen, and will most likely drop and grow in size. Using a slightly smaller needle than the usual recommended size for the yarn ensures that the knitted fabric retains its shape.

Gauge (tension) can differ quite dramatically between knitters. This is because of the way that the needles and the yarn are held. So if your gauge (tension) does not match that stated in the pattern, you should change your needle size following this simple rule:
- If your knitting is too loose, your gauge (tension) will read that you have fewer stitches and rows than the given gauge (tension), and you will need to change to a smaller needle to make the stitch size smaller.
- If your knitting is too tight, your gauge (tension) will read that you have more stitches

and rows than the given gauge (tension), and you will need to change to a thicker needle to make the stitch size bigger.

Please note that if the projects in this book are not knitted to the correct gauge (tension), yarn quantities will be affected.

Knitting a gauge swatch

No matter how excited you are about a new knitting project and how annoying it seems to have to spend time knitting a gauge swatch before you start, please do take the time, as it will not be wasted.

Use the same needles, yarn and stitch pattern as those that will be used for the main work and knit a sample at least 5 in. (12.5 cm) square. Smooth out the finished piece on a flat surface, but do not stretch it.

To check the stitch gauge, place a ruler horizontally on the sample, measure 4 in. (10 cm) across and mark with a pin at each end. Count the number of stitches between the pins. To check the row gauge, place a ruler vertically on the sample, measure 4 in. (10 cm) and mark with pins. Count the number of rows between the pins. If the number of stitches and rows is greater then specified in the pattern, make a new swatch using larger needles; if it is less, make a new swatch using smaller needles.

abbreviations

beg	beginning/begin
cont	continue
cm	centimeter
C4B	cable 4 back: slip next 2 sts onto a cable needle and hold at back of work, k2, then k2 from the cable needle
C4F	cable 4 front: slip next 2 sts onto a cable needle and hold at front of work, k2, then k2 from the cable needle
C6B	cable 6 back: slip next 3 sts onto a cable needle and hold at back of work, k3, then k3 from the cable needle
dec	decrease
g	grams
in	inch
inc	increase
K	knit
K2tog	knit two stitches together.
K2togtbl	knit 2 stitches together through the back of the loop
K3tog	knit three stitches together
MB	make bobble: (k1, p1) twice into next st, (turn, p4, turn, k4) twice, turn, p4, turn and sl2, k2tog, psso
mm	millimeter
M1	make one stitch
ML	make loop as follows: Knit into next stitch and before slipping the stitch off the left needle, bring yarn to the front of the work between the needle points

	and wrap around your thumb to create loop and then back through the needle points. Knit into the stitch again and then slip off needle. You will now have two stitches on the right hand needle. Cast off one stitch by lifting one over the other.
oz	ounces
P	purl
P2sso	pass two slipped stitches over
P2togtbl	purl 2 stitches together through the back of the loop
patt	pattern
PB	place bead: yarn forward, slip bead to front of work, slip 1 st purlwise, take yarn to back of work. Bead will now be sitting in front of slipped stitch
psso	pass slipped stitch over
P2tog	purl two stitches together
rep	repeat
RS	right side of work
sl	slip
St st	stockinette (stocking) stitch
st/sts	stitch/stitches
WS	wrong side of work
yb	yarn back
yfwd	yarn forward
YO	yarn over
*	repeat instructions between * as many times as instructed
( )	repeat instructions between ( ) as many times as instructed.

holding the yarn and needles

Before casting on it is a good idea to get used to holding the yarn and needles.
Remember, they are bound to feel really awkward at first.

Holding the needles

1 The right needle is held in the same way as a pencil (English). When casting on and working the first few rows the knitted piece passes over the hand, between the thumb and the index finger. As the work progresses, let the thumb slide under the knitted piece and hold the needle from below.

2 The left needle is held lightly over the top. If using the English method of knitting (main picture), the thumb and index finger control the tip of the needle. If using the Continental method (see inset,) control the tip with the thumb and middle finger.

Holding the yarn

There are several ways of winding the yarn around your fingers to control the tension; here are two of the simplest.

Method one
To hold the yarn in your right hand, pass it under your little finger, over your third finger, under your middle finger and over your index finger. Your index finger is used to pass the yarn around the tip of the needle. The tension on the yarn is controlled by gripping the yarn in the crook of the little finger.

Method two
To hold the yarn in your right hand (left hand if using the Continental method, see inset), pass it under your little finger, then around this finger, over your third finger, under your center finger and over your index finger. Your index finger is used to pass the yarn around the tip of the needle. The yarn circled around your little finger creates the necessary tension for even knitting.

making a slipknot

A slipknot is the basis of all casting on techniques (see page 14) and is therefore the starting point for almost everything you do in knitting.

1 Wind the yarn around two fingers twice as shown. Insert a knitting needle through the first (front) strand and under the second (back) one.

2 Using the needle, pull the back strand through the front one to form a loop.

3 Holding the loose ends of the yarn with your left hand, pull the needle upwards, thus tightening the knot. Pull the ball end of the yarn again to tighten the knot further.

tips

Getting started
The yarn may be held in either the right or left hand; the two ways are referred to as the English and the Continental methods. Try holding the yarn in either of the ways shown opposite, though you may well develop a personal method. Ideally, ask a knitter to cast on a few stitches for you as it is easier to handle the yarn and needles with some stitches already cast on.

I usually use the cable method of casting on (see page 15). The cable method of casting on gives a firm, neat finish and is ideal for ribs.

If you knit very tightly you may need to use a larger needle size to cast on.

casting on

Casting on is the term used for making a row of stitches to be used as a foundation for your knitting. There are several methods of casting on which produce different kinds of edges, but here are two examples, the cable method being my preferred option.

Thumb method

1 Make a slip knot 40 in. (100 cm) from the end of the yarn. Hold the needle in your right hand with the ball end of the yarn over your index finger. *Wind the loose end of the yarn around your left thumb from front to back.

2 Insert the point of the needle under the first strand of yarn on your thumb.

3 With your right index finger, take the ball end of the yarn over the point of the needle.

4 Pull a loop through to form the first stitch. Remove your left thumb from the yarn. Pull the loose end to secure the stitch (see inset). Repeat from * until the required number of stitches have been cast on.

Cable method

1 This method of casting on requires two needles. Make a slipknot about 4 in. (10 cm) from the end of the yarn. Hold this needle in your left hand.

2 Insert the right-hand needle through the slipknot. Wrap the yarn over the point of the right-hand needle.

3 Pull a loop through the slipknot with the right-hand needle.

4 Place this loop on the left-hand needle. Gently pull the yarn to secure the stitch.

5 Insert the right-hand needle between the slip knot and the first stitch on the left-hand needle. Wrap the yarn round the point of the right-hand needle.

6 Draw a loop through, place this loop on the left-hand needle. Repeat steps 5 and 6 until the required number of stitches have been cast on.

the basic stitches

The knit and purl stitches form the basis of all knitted fabrics. The knit stitch is the easiest to learn and once you have mastered this you can move on to the purl stitch, which is the reverse of the knit stitch.

Knit stitch

1 Hold the needle with the cast-on stitches in your left hand, with the loose yarn at the back of the work. Insert the right-hand needle from left to right through the front of the first stitch on the left-hand needle.

2 Wrap the yarn from left to right over the point of the right-hand needle.

3 Draw the yarn through the stitch, thus forming a new stitch on the right-hand needle.

4 Slip the original stitch off the left-hand needle, keeping the new stitch on the right-hand needle.

5 To knit a row, repeat steps 1 to 4 until all the stitches have been transferred from the left-hand needle to the right-hand needle. Turn the work, transferring the needle with the stitches to your left hand to work the next row.

Purl stitch

1 Hold the needle with the stitches in your left hand, with the loose yarn at the front of the work. Insert the right-hand needle from right to left into the front of the first stitch on the left-hand needle.

2 Wrap the yarn from right to left, up and over the point of the right-hand needle.

3 Draw the yarn through the stitch, thus forming a new stitch on the right-hand needle.

4 Slip the original stitch off the left-hand needle, keeping the new stitch on the right-hand needle.

5 To purl a row, repeat steps 1 to 4 until all the stitches have been transferred from the left-hand needle to the right-hand needle. Turn the work, transferring the needle with the stitches to your left hand to work the next row.

intarsia stitches

Intarsia is the name given to color knitting where the pattern is worked in large blocks of color at a time, requiring a separate ball of yarn for each area of color as the yarn must not be stranded across the back.

Diagonal color change with a slant to the left

This diagram shows a color change on the wrong side of the work.

Use separate balls of yarn for each block of color. On a right side row, with the yarns at the back of the work, the crossing of colors at joins happens automatically because of the encroaching nature of the pattern. On a wrong side row, with the yarns at the front of the work, take the first color over the second color, drop it then pick up the second color underneath the first color thus crossing the two colors together.

Diagonal color change with a slant to the right

This diagram shows a color change on the right side of the work.

Use separate balls of yarn for each block of color. On a right side row, with the yarns at the back of the work, take the first color over the second color, drop it then pick up the second color underneath the first color thus crossing the two colors. On a wrong side row, with the yarns at the front of the work, the crossing of the two colors at the joins happens automatically because of the encroaching nature of the pattern.

Vertical color change

This diagram shows a color change on the wrong side of the work.

Use separate balls of yarn for each block of color. Work in the first color to the color change, then drop the first color, pick up the second color underneath the first color, crossing the two colors over before working the next stitch in the second color. Work the first stitch after a color change is worked firmly to avoid a gap forming between colors. This technique ensures that the yarns are crossed on every row and gives a neat vertical line between colors on the right side, and a vertical line of loops in each color on the wrong side.

fair isle stitches

Stranding is used when the yarn not in use is left at the back of the work until needed. The loops formed by stranding are called "floats" and it is important to ensure that they are not pulled too tightly when working the next stitch as this will pull in your knitting.

Stranding

1 On a knit row, hold the first color in your right hand and the second color in your left hand. Knit the required number of stitches as usual with the first color, carrying the second color loosely across the wrong side of the work.

2 To knit a stitch in the second color, insert the right-hand needle into the next stitch then draw a loop through from the yarn held in the left hand, carrying the yarn in the right hand loosely across the wrong side until required.

3 On a purl row, hold the yarns as for the knit rows. Purl the required number of stitches as usual with the first color, carrying the second color loosely across these stitches on the wrong side of the work.

4 To purl a stitch in the second color, insert the right-hand needle into the next stitch then draw a loop through from the yarn held in the left hand, carrying the yarn in the right hand loosely across the wrong side until next required.

increasing and decreasing

Many projects will require some shaping, either just to add interest or to allow them to fit comfortably. Shaping is achieved by increasing or decreasing the number of stiches you are working.

Increasing

The simplest method of increasing one stitch is to work into the front and back of the same stitch.

On a knit row, knit into the front of the stitch to be increased into, then before slipping it off the needle, place the right-hand needle behind the left-hand one and knit again into the back of it (inc). Slip the original stitch off the left-hand needle.

On a purl row, purl into the front of the stitch to be increased into, then before slipping it off the needle, purl again into the back of it. Slip the original stitch off the left-hand needle.

Decreasing

The simplest method of decreasing one stitch is to work two stitches together.

On a knit row, insert the right-hand needle from left to right through two stitches instead of one, then knit them together as one stitch. This is called knit two together (K2tog).

On a purl row, insert the right-hand needle from right to left through two stitches instead of one, then purl them together as one stitch. This is called purl two together (P2tog).

binding·off

This is the most commonly-used method of securing stitches once you have finished a piece of knitting. The bound-off edge should have the same "give" or elasticity as the fabric and you should bind off in the stitch used for the main fabric unless the pattern directs otherwise.

Knitwise

Knit two stitches. *Using the point of the left-hand needle lift the first stitch on the right-hand needle over the second then drop it off the needle. Knit the next stitch and repeat from * until all stitches have been worked off the left-hand needle and only one stitch remains on the right-hand needle. Cut the yarn, leaving enough to sew in the end, thread the end through the stitch then slip it off the needle. Draw the yarn up firmly to fasten off.

Purlwise

Purl two stitches. *Using the point of the left-hand needle lift the first stitch on the right-hand needle over the second and drop it off the needle. Purl the next stitch and repeat from * until all the stitches have been worked off the left-hand needle and only one stitch remains on the right-hand needle. Secure the last stitch as described in binding off knitwise.

tips

Binding off
The excitement of arriving at the last stage of your knitting can make you bind off without taking the same care that you have used in the rest of the work.

You should take into account the part of the project you are working on. If you are a tight knitter you may need to bind off with a larger needle, or if you are a loose knitter bind off with a smaller needle.

Lace stitches should also be bound off in pattern, slipping, making stitches, or decreasing as you go, to make sure that the fabric doesn't widen or gather up.

project index

Here's a gallery of all the specially designed projects featured in the book. They use a range of interesting new yarns to help create a truly unique look. Once you have become familiar with the basic techniques, you'll find all these projects easy and fun to make.

floral

Worked in a simple A-line shape, this ultra feminine bag is deceptively easy to knit. Super cotton and nubby tweed create plenty of texture, and vibrant floral accents add a dash of whimsy.

Materials

Yarn A Two 50g balls of Rowan Handknit Cotton, Color 219 Gooseberry

Yarn B Two 50g balls of Rowan Yorkshire Tweed DK, Color 348 Lime Leaf

Yarn C One 50g ball of Rowan All Seasons Cotton, Color 216 Citron

US 6 (4 mm) needles

US 10 (6 mm) needles

Lining fabric, approx. 24 × 24 in. (60 × 60 cm)

One small magnetic snap (optional)

Gauge

14 sts and 20 rows to 4 in. (10 cm) using one strand of A and one strand of B on US 10 (6 mm) needles measured over stockinette stitch.

Finished size: 10½ × 8 in. (26.5 × 20 cm)

Front and Back (make 1 of each)

Cast on 37 sts using one strand of A and one strand of B held together on US 10 (6 mm) needles.

Row 1: (RS) Knit.

Row 2: (WS) Purl.

Repeat last 2 rows once more, ending with a WS row.

Row 5: K2tog, knit to last 2 sts, K2tog. (35 sts)

Row 6: Purl.

Row 7: Knit.

Row 8: Purl.

Row 9: Knit.

Row 10: Purl.

Row 11: K2tog, knit to last 2 sts, K2tog. (33 sts)

Repeat rows 6–11 four more times, ending with a RS row. (25 sts)

Next: Purl.

Next: Knit.

Repeat last 2 rows once more, ending with a RS row.

Next: Knit. (This creates garter stitch ridge for turn over at top of bag.)

Next: Knit.

Next: Purl.
Repeat last 2 rows once more, ending with a
  WS row.
Bind off.

Handle

Cast on 5 sts using one strand of A and one strand
  of B held together on US 10 (6 mm) needles.
Row 1: (RS) Knit.
Row 2: (WS) K1, P3, K1.
Repeat last 2 rows until handle measures 13 in.
  (32 cm) from cast-on edge, ending with a WS
  row.
Bind off.

Flowers (make 5)

Make two flowers using A, two using C, and one
using B as follows:
Cast on 93 sts using US 6 (4 mm) needles.
Row 1: K1, *K2, lift first of these sts over second,
  rep from * to end. (47 sts)
Row 2: P1, (P2tog) to end. (24 sts)
Row 3: Knit.
Row 4: Purl.

Break off yarn, thread through remaining sts and
pull together. Twist frill around into a flower shape
and secure using the yarn still attached.

Finishing

Using the mattress stitch, sew together the front
and back of the bag by working down one side,
across the bottom and up the other side.

Make fabric lining as follows:
Using the knitted bag as a template, cut two pieces
of lining fabric slightly larger than the knitted
pieces plus ³⁄₈ in. (1 cm) at the sides and the
bottom for the seam allowance. Sew the two
pieces together by stitching down one side, across
the bottom and up the other side. Turn the knitted
bag inside out and with the lining fabric also inside
out, sew the bottom two corners of the lining to
the bottom two corners of the knitted bag. Keeping
the bag inside out, turn the lining back over the
bag—it will look as if the whole bag has been
turned inside out. Slip stitch the hems at the top of
the bag into place, at the same time securing and
covering the top edges of the lining. Turn the bag
the right side out.

Sew handle into place inside the bag at the top of
side seams and sew a magnetic snap fastening into
place at top center of the bag if desired. Sew
flowers into place using the photograph as a guide.

angel

This modern, everyday handbag is created using some simple shaping and is accentuated with garter-stitch ridges. The delicate texture of the flower and leaves offer a pretty contrast.

Materials

Yarn A Three 50g balls of Rowan All Seasons Cotton, Color 192 Iceberg

Yarn B One 50g ball of Rowan 4 ply Soft, Color 377 Wink

Yarn C One 25g ball of Rowan Kidsilk Haze, Color 583 Blushes (used double)

Yarn D One 50g ball of Rowan Yorkshire Tweed DK, Color 349 Frog

US 3 (3.25 mm) needles

US 7 (4.5 mm) needles

Lining fabric, approx. 32 × 32 in. (80 × 80 cm)

One small magnetic snap (optional)

Stitch marker

Gauge

18 sts and 25 rows to 4 in. (10 cm) using A on US 7 (4.5 mm) needles measured over stockinette stitch.

Finished size: 16 1/2 in. (41.5 cm) measured around

Front and Back (make 1 of each)

Cast on 45 sts using A and US 7 (4.5 mm) needles.

Row 1: (RS) Knit.

Row 2: (WS) Purl.

Row 3: Knit.

Repeat last 2 rows twice more, ending with a RS row.

Row 8: Knit. (This creates garter stitch ridge for turn over at top of bag.)

Row 9: Knit.

Row 10: Purl.

Repeat last 2 rows three more times, ending with a WS row.

Place markers on the 5th, 14th, 23rd, 32nd and 41st sts. You should have five marked sts in total.

Row 17: (inc row) K4, M1, knit marked st, M1 (K8, M1, knit marked st, M1) to last 4 sts, K4. (55 sts)

Row 18: Purl.

Row 19: Knit.

Repeat last row three more times, ending with a WS row.

Row 23: (inc row) K5, M1, knit marked st, M1 (K10, M1, knit marked st, M1) to last 5 sts, K5. (65 sts)

Row 24: Knit.

Repeat last row four more times, ending with a WS row.

Row 29: (inc row) K6, M1, knit marked st, M1 (K12, M1, knit marked st, M1) to last 6 sts, K6. (75 sts)

Row 30: Knit.

Repeat last row four more times, ending with a WS row.

Row 35: (dec row) K5, K2tog, knit marked st, K2tog (K10, K2tog, knit marked st, K2tog) to last 5 sts, K5. (65 sts)

Row 36: Knit.

Repeat last row four more times, ending with a WS row.

Row 41: (dec row) K4, K2tog, knit marked st, K2tog (K8, K2tog, knit marked st, K2tog) to last 4 sts, K4. (55 sts)

Row 42: Knit.

Repeat last row four more times, ending with a WS row.

Row 47: (dec row) K3, K2tog, knit marked st, K2tog (K6, K2tog, knit marked st, K2tog) to last 3 sts, K3. (45 sts)

Row 48: Knit.

Repeat last row twice more, ending with a WS row.

Row 51: (dec row) K2, K2tog, knit marked st, K2tog (K4, K2tog, knit marked st, K2tog) to last 2 sts, K2. (35 sts)

Row 52: Knit.

Bind off.

Handle (make 2)

Cast on 7 sts, using A and US 7 (4.5 mm) needles.

Row 1: (RS) Knit.

Row 2: (WS) K1, P5, K1.

Repeat last 2 rows until work measures 14 in. (35 cm) from cast-on edge, ending with a WS row. Bind off.

Flowers (make 3)

Cast on 73 sts using C and US 3 (3.25 mm) needles.

Change to B.

Row 1: K1, *K2, lift first of these sts over second, rep from * to end. (37 sts)

Row 2: P1, (P2tog) to end. (19 sts)

Break off yarn, thread through remaining stitches and pull together. Twist frill around into a flower shape and secure, using the yarn still attached.

Leaves (make 4)

Cast on 3 sts using D and US 3 (3.25 mm) needles.

Row 1: K1, P1, K1.

Row 2: K1, M1, K1, M1, K1. (5 sts)

Row 3: K1, P3, K1.

Row 4: K2, M1, K1, M1, K2. (7 sts)

Row 5: K1, P5, K1.

Row 6: K3, M1, K1, M1, K3. (9 sts)

Row 7: K1, P7, K1.

Row 8: K3, sl2, K1, p2sso, K3. (7 sts)

Row 9: K1, P5, K1.

Row 10: K2, sl2, K1, p2sso, K2. (5 sts)

Row 11: K1, P3, K1.

Row 12: K1, sl2, K1, p2sso, K1. (3 sts)

Row 13: K1, P1, K1.

Row 14: Sl2, K1, p2sso. (1 st)

Fasten off.

Finishing

Using the mattress stitch, sew the font and back of the bag together by working down one side, across the bottom and up the other side.

Make fabric lining as follows:

> ### note
> As this is a shaped bag, the pieces of fabric lining need to be considerably larger than the knitted pieces so that the lining can "fill out" inside the bag.

Using the knitted bag as a template, cut two pieces of lining fabric larger than the knitted pieces plus 3/8 in. (1 cm) at the sides and the bottom for the seam allowance. Sew the two pieces together by working down one side, across the bottom and up the other side. Turn the knitted bag inside out and with the lining fabric also inside out, sew the bottom two corners of the lining to the bottom two corners of the knitted bag. Keeping the knitted bag inside out, turn the lining back over the bag—it will look as if the whole bag has been turned inside out. Slip stitch hems at the top of the bag in place, at the same time securing and covering the top edges of the lining. Turn the bag right side out.

Sew a magnetic snap fastening into place at top center of the bag if desired.

Sew flowers and leaves into place using photograph as a guide.

Sew the handles to the top of the bag, 1 1/4 in. (3 cm) in from each side seam.

mango

Style and practicality team up to make this easy-going tote an ideal everyday carry-all. Oversized cables and bobbles knit in chunky yarn lend maximum textural interest, while an eye-popping palette gives it a contemporary edge.

Materials

Yarn A Two 100g balls of Rowan Big Wool, Color 029 Pistachio

Yarn B Two 100g balls of Rowan Ribbon Twist, Color 111 Ribble

US 17 (12 mm) needles

Cable needle

Lining fabric, approx. 32 × 32 in. (80 × 80 cm)

One large magnetic snap (optional)

Gauge

10 sts and 11 rows to 4 in. (10 cm) on US 17 (12 mm) needles measured over cable pattern.

Finished size: 13 × 12 in. (32 × 30 cm)

Abbreviations

MB Make Bobble: Using B, knit into the front, back and front of next st (3 sts), turn P3, turn K3, turn P3, turn sl 1, K2tog, psso.

C4B Cable 4 Back: Slip next 2 sts onto cable needle and hold at back of work, K2 sts from left-hand needle, then K2 sts from cable needle.

Front

Cast on 32 sts with A and US 17 (12 mm) needles.

Row 1: (RS) P5 (K4, P5) to end.

Row 2: (WS) K5 (P4, K5) to end.

Repeat last 2 rows once more ending with a WS row.

Row 5: P2, MB, P2, (K4, P2, MB, P2) to end.

Row 6: Work as row 2.

Row 7: P5, (C4B, P5) to end.

Row 8: Work as row 2.

Row 9: Work as row 1.

Row 10: Work as row 2.

Rep rows 5–10 three more times and then repeat rows 5–8 again, ending with a WS row.

Next: Purl. (This creates garter st ridge for turn over at top of bag.)

Change to B.

Next: Purl.

Next: Knit.

Next: Purl.

Bind off.

Back

Work as for the front, omitting bobbles.

Base

Cast on 8 sts with B and US 17 (12 mm) needles.

Row 1: (RS) Knit.

Row 2: (WS) Purl.

Repeat last 2 rows until work measures 13 in. (32 cm) from cast-on edge, ending with a WS row (or until base will fit neatly along the cast-on edges of the front and back).

Bind off.

Sides and handle (knitted in one piece)

Cast on 8 sts with B and US 17 (12 mm) needles.

Row 1: (RS) Knit.

Row 2: (WS) K1, P6, K1.

Repeat last 2 rows until work measures 42 in. (105 cm) from cast-on edge, ending with a WS row.

Bind off.

Finishing

Using the mattress stitch, sew the side edges of the base to the cast-on edges of the front and back. Sew the cast-on edge of the side/handle to the left hand end of the base, and the bound-off edge to the right-hand end of the base.

Make fabric lining as follows:

Using the knitted bag as a template, cut two pieces of fabric slightly larger than the front and back, plus 3/8 in. (1 cm) at sides and bottom for seams. Do the same for the base and two sides, allowing 3/8 in. (1 cm) all around. Make a 3/8 in. (1 cm) seam across the top of the two side pieces, as they will be seen. Sew the lining together as for the knitted pieces. Turn the bag inside out, and with the lining also inside out, sew the bottom four corners of the lining to the bottom four corners of the bag. Turn the lining back over the bag. Slip stitch the lining at the top of the bag into place, covering the top edges of the lining. Turn the bag right side out.

Sew a magnetic snap fastening inside the top center of the bag if desired.

violet

A shapely little evening purse with glittering bead detail is perfect for a night on the town. Knitting with beads is a great way of adding a hint of sophistication and glamour. Once you have seen how simple it is to do, you'll be applying beads on everything!

Materials
One 50g ball of Rowan Cotton Glace,
  Color 787 Hyacinth
US 3 (3.25 mm) needles
Approx. 143 purple beads, 3 mm (J3001014)

Gauge
23 sts and 32 rows to 4 in. (10 cm) on US 3 (3.25 mm) needles measured over stockinette stitch.

Finished size: 6¾ (widest point at top) × 7¼ in. (17 × 18 cm)

Abbreviation
PB Place Bead: WYIF, slip bead to front of work, sl 1 purlwise, take yarn to back of work. The bead will now be sitting in front of the slipped stitch (see "Knitting with beads" page 80).

Front
Cast on 39 sts using US 3 (3.25 mm) needles.
Row 1: (RS) Knit.
This row forms garter stitch. Repeat this row 11 more times, ending with a WS row.
Row 13: Knit.
Row 14: Purl.
Row 15: (eyelet row) K4 (YO, K2tog, K4) to last 5 sts, YO, K2tog, K3.
Row 16: Purl.
Row 17: Knit.

Row 18: Purl.*
Row 19: K1, PB, (K5, PB) to last st, K1.
Row 20: Purl.
Row 21: Knit.
Row 22: Purl.
Row 23: K4, PB, (K5, PB) to last 4 sts, K4.
Row 24: Purl.
Row 25: Knit.
Row 26: Purl.
Rows 19–26 form the pattern. Repeat these rows 4 more times and then repeat row 19 once more, ending with a RS row.
**Next: Purl.
Next: K2, sl 1, K1, psso (k3, sl 1, K1, psso) to last 5 sts, K2, sl 1, K1, psso, K1. (31 sts)
Next: Purl.
Next: K2, sl 1, K1, psso (K2, sl 1, K1, psso) to last 3 sts, K3. (24 sts)
Next: Purl.
Next: K2, sl 1, K1, psso (K1, sl 1, K1, psso) to last 2 sts, K2. (17 sts)
Next: Purl.
Next: K1, (sl 1, K1, psso) to end. (9 sts)
Next: Purl.
Next: K1 (sl 1, K1, psso) to end. (5 sts)
Do not bind off. Break off yarn and thread through remaining sts and pull together.

Back
Work as for front until * and then as follows:
Row 19: K4, PB (K5, PB) to last 4 sts, K4.

Row 20: Purl.
Row 21: Knit.
Row 22: Purl.
Row 23: K1, PB (K5, PB) to last st, K1.
Row 24: Purl.
Row 25: Knit.
Row 26: Purl.
Rows 19–26 form the pattern. Repeat these rows 4 more times and then repeat row 19 once more, ending with a RS row.
Now work as for front from ** to end.

Handle
Make a twisted cord as follows: Cut 2 lengths of yarn approx. 50 in. (125 cm) long and knot them together at each end. Ask someone to hold one end of the yarn while you hold the other. With the yarn stretched out, twist the ends in opposite directions until the cord begins to twist back on itself. Bring the two ends together and hold tightly, allowing the two halves to twist together. You now have a twisted cord approximately 20 in. (50 cm) long. Knot ends and smooth.

Finishing
Using the mattress stitch, sew the front and back of the bag together by working down one side, around the bottom and up the other side.

Thread the twisted cord through the eyelets, bringing ends out to tie.

ballerina

The fuzzy, ruffled edge offers a softness and balance to the textured rib of this elongated handbag. A knotted handle is an unusual, yet simple, addition.

Materials
Yarn A One 25g ball of Rowan Kidsilk Haze, Color 583 Blushes (used double)
Yarn B One 50g ball of Rowan Yorkshire Tweed DK, Color 350 Frolic
US 6 (4 mm) needles
Lining fabric, approx. 14 × 20 in. (36 × 50 cm)
One small magnetic snap (optional)

Gauge
21 sts and 30 rows to 4 in. (10 cm) using B on US 6 (4 mm) needles measured over pattern.

Finished size: $5^7/_8 \times 8^3/_4$ in. (14.75 × 22 cm)

Front and Back (make 1 of each)
Cast on 121 sts using A and US 6 (4 mm) needles.
Row 1: (RS) K1, (K2, lift first of these over second) to end. (61 sts)
Row 2: (WS) P1, (P2tog) to end. (31 sts)
Row 3: Knit.
Row 4: Purl.
Change to B.
Row 5: Knit.
Row 6: (K1, P1) to last st, K1.
Repeat last 2 rows until work measures $8^3/_4$ in. (22 cm) from beginning of row 5, ending with a WS row.
Bind off.

Handle (make 2)
Cast on 5 sts using B and US 6 (4 mm) needles.
Row 1: (RS) Knit.
Row 2: (WS) K1, P3, K1.
Repeat last 2 rows until handle measures 12 in. (30 cm) from cast-on edge, ending with a WS row.
Bind off.

Finishing
Using the mattress stitch, sew the front and back of the bag together by working down one side, across the bottom and up the other side. Sew the bound-off edge of one of the handles to the inside of the bag, at the top of the left side seam. Then sew the bound-off edge of the other handle to the inside of the bag at the top of the right side seam.

Make fabric lining as follows:
Using the knitted bag as a template, cut out two pieces of lining fabric slightly larger than the knitted pieces plus $^3/_8$ in. (1 cm) all the way around for the seam allowance. Sew a $^3/_8$ in. (1 cm) hem across the top edges of both pieces to neaten them up, since they will be seen. Sew the two pieces together by working down one side, across the bottom and up the other side.

Turn the knitted bag inside out. With the lining fabric also inside out, sew the bottom two corners of the lining to the bottom two corners of the knitted bag. Keeping the knitted bag inside out, turn the fabric lining back over the bag. It will now look as if the whole bag has been turned inside out. Slip stitch the lining into place around the top of the bag. Turn the bag the right way out.

Sew a magnetic snap in place at the top center of bag, if desired. Tie the two cast-on edges of the handles together with a knot.

mulberry

Mohair and tweed work together to create a very soft knit in this satchel-style bag. A garter-stitch "belt" with buckle fastening makes a quirky addition.

Materials

Yarn A Two 50g balls of Rowan Felted Tweed, Color 151 Bilberry

Yarn B Two 50g balls of Rowan Kid Classic, Color 835 Royal

US 8 (5 mm) needles

US 6 (4 mm) needles

One purple buckle (Rowan 00361), 1 ½ x 2 ¼ in. (4 x 6 cm)

Lining fabric, approx. 24 × 24 in. (60 × 60 cm)

One small magnetic snap (optional)

Gauge

17 sts and 24 rows to 4 in. (10 cm) using one strand of A and one strand of B held together and US 8 (5 mm) needles measured over stockinette stitch.

Finished size: 10½ × 9¼ in. (26.5 × 23 cm)

Front and Back (make one of each)

Cast on 45 sts using one strand of A and one strand of B and US 8 (5 mm) needles.

Row 1: (RS) Knit.

Row 2: (WS) Purl.

Repeat last 2 rows until work measures 9¼ in. (23 cm) from cast-on edge, ending with a RS row.

Next: Knit. (This creates a garter st ridge for turn over at top of bag.)

Next: Knit.

Next: Purl.

Repeat last 2 rows once more, ending with a WS row.

Bind off.

Sides, base, and handle (knitted all in one piece)

Cast on 7 sts using B and US 6 (4 mm) needles.

Row 1: (RS) Knit.

Repeat this row until work measures 48 in. (120 cm) from cast-on edge, ending with WS row.

Bind off.

Belt

Cast on 13 sts using B and US 6 (4 mm) needles.

Row 1: (RS) Knit.

Repeat this row until work measures 25 ½ in. (64 cm) from cast-on edge, ending with WS row.

Bind off.

Finishing

Join the cast-on edge of the sides/base/handle to the bound-off edge. With the join at the center of the base, use mattress stitch to sew the base section of the sides/base/handle to the cast-on edges of the front and back of the bag. Sew the rest of the sides/handle into position.

Make fabric lining as follows:

Using the knitted bag as a template, cut out two pieces of lining fabric slightly larger than the front and back pieces, plus ⅜ in. (1 cm) seam allowance at the side and bottom edges. Do the same for the base and two sides, but allowing ⅜ in. (1 cm) for the seam all the way around. The two pieces of fabric that are to line the sides must be given a ⅜ in. (1 cm) seam across the top to neaten them up as they will be seen. Sew the lining together as you did for the knitted pieces. Turn the knitted bag inside out and with the lining fabric also inside out, sew the bottom four corners of the lining to the bottom four corners of the knitted bag. Keeping the knitted bag inside out, turn the fabric lining back over the bag. It will now look as if the whole bag has been turned inside out. Slip stitch the knitted hems at the top of the bag into place, securing and covering the top edges of the lining. Turn the bag the right side out.

Sew a magnetic snap into place at the top center of the bag if desired.

Thread the bound-off edge of the belt around the middle post of the buckle and slip stitch into place. Now the buckle is attached to the belt; position and fasten belt around the bag using the photograph as a guide. Slip stitch belt into place neatly and securely.

spearmint

This spirited zigzag scarf achieves its striking geometric shape with basic increasing and decreasing. Stripes of mohair and Lurex Shimmer are echoed in the long tassels at the ends.

Materials

Yarn A Two 50g balls of Rowan Yorkshire Tweed DK, Color 347 Skip

Yarn B One 25g ball of Rowan Kidsilk Haze, Color 582 Trance

Yarn C One 25g ball of Rowan Lurex Shimmer, Color 333 Pewter

US 6 (4 mm) needles

Large crochet hook

Gauge

22 sts and 30 rows to 4 in. (10 cm) using A on US 6 (4 mm) needles measured over stockinette stitch.

Finished size: 5 × 60 in. (12.5 × 150 cm)

Scarf

Cast on 1 st using A and US 6 (4 mm) needles.

Row 1: (RS) Increase into st. (2 sts)

Row 2: (WS) Increase into first st, K1. (3 sts)

Row 3: Knit.

Row 4: Knit.

Row 5: K1, M1, knit to last st, M1, K1. (5 sts)

Repeat last 2 rows until 27 sts, ending with a RS row.

Next: Knit.

Next: K1, K2togtbl, knit to last 3 sts, K2tog, K1. (25 sts)

Next: Knit.

Repeat last 2 rows until 11 sts, ending with a WS row.

*Change to one strand of B and one strand of C.

Next: Knit.

Repeat last row 3 more times, ending with a WS row.

Change to A.

Next: Knit.

Next: Knit.

Next: K1, M1, knit to last st, M1, K1. (13 sts)

Repeat last 2 rows until 27 sts, ending with a RS row.

Next: Knit.

Next: K1, K2togtbl, knit to last 3 sts, K2tog, K1. (25 sts)

Next: Knit.

Repeat last 2 rows until 11 sts, ending with a WS row.

Repeat from * 10 more times, ending with a WS row.

Change to one strand of B and one strand of C.

Next: Knit.

Repeat last row 3 more times, ending with a WS row.

Change to A.

Next: Knit.

Next: Knit.

Next: K1, M1, knit to last st, M1, K1. (13 sts)

Repeat last 2 rows until 27 sts, ending with a RS row.

Next: Knit.

Next: K1, K2togtbl, knit to last 3 sts, K2tog, K1. (25 sts)

Next: Knit.

Repeat last 2 rows until 5 . ending with a WS row.

Next: K1, K3tog, K1. (3 sts)

Next: Knit.

Next: Sl 2, K1, p2sso.

Fasten off.

Tassels (make 2)

Cut 17 in. (42 cm) lengths of yarn as follows: 2 lengths of A, 4 lengths of B and 2 lengths of C. Hold all 8 strands of yarn together and fold in half. Using a large crochet hook, thread the folded loop through the cast-on edge at the point of the first diamond, pull the ends through the loop and then pull them to secure the tassel. Make another tassel the same way and join at the bound-off edge at the point of the last diamond.

fizz

A bold ruffle and wide rib combine to create this eye-catching, short scarf. A narrow opening at one end allows you to tuck the other end of the scarf through for a snug fit.

Materials

Yarn A One 50g ball of Rowan Wool Cotton, Color 958 Aloof (used double)
Yarn B Two 50g hanks of Rowan Summer Tweed, Color 527 Sprig
US 8 (5 mm) needles
2 stitch holders
Spare knitting needle

Gauge

16 sts and 23 rows to 4 in. (10 cm) using B on US 8 (5 mm) needles measured over stockinette stitch.

Finished size: 8³/₄ × 32 in. (21.75 × 80 cm)

First panel

Cast on 137 sts using A (used double) and US 8 (5mm) needles.
Row 1: (RS) K1, (K2, lift first of these over second) to end. (69 sts)
Row 2: (WS) P1, (P2tog) to end. (35 sts)
Change to B.
Row 3: K4, P3, (K3, P3) to last 4 sts, K4.
Row 4: K1, P3, (K3, P3) to last st, K1.
Repeat last 2 rows 8 more times, ending with a WS row.
Divide for slit as follows:
Next row: K4, (P3, K3) twice, P1, K1, turn.
Next row: Bind off one st, then (P3, K3) twice, P3, K1. (17 sts, including st used to bind off)
Next row: K4, (P3, K3) twice, K1.

Next row: K1, (P3, K3) twice, P3, K1.
Repeat last 2 rows 10 more times, ending with a WS row.
Next row: K4, (P3, K3) twice, K1.
Leave these 17 sts on a holder. Break off yarn.
With RS facing, rejoin yarn to remaining 17 sts and work as follows:
Next row: (RS) K1, (K3, P3) twice, K4.
Next row: (WS) K1, (P3, K3) twice, P3, K1.
Repeat last 2 rows 11 more times, ending with a WS row.
Next row: K1, (K3, P3) twice, K4.
You will now have two sections of knitting. Join these two sections as follows:
Next row: K1 (P3, K3) twice, P3, K1, cast on 1 st, and then (working across the 17 sts on the holder), K1, (P3, K3) twice, P3, K1. (35 sts)
The two sections are now joined and you will have all 35 sts back onto one needle.
Continue as follows:
Next row: K4, P3, (K3, P3) to last 4 sts, K4.
Next row: K1, P3, (K3, P3) to last st, K1.
Repeat last 2 rows until scarf measures 16 in. (40 cm) from cast-on edge, ending with a WS row.
Do not bind off. Leave sts on a holder.

Second panel

Cast on 137 sts using A (used double) and US 8 (5 mm) needles.
Row 1: (RS) K1, (K2, lift first of these sts over second) to end. (69 sts)
Row 2: (WS) P1, (P2tog) to end. (35 sts)
Change to B.
Row 3: K4, P3, (K3, P3) to last 4 sts, K4.
Row 4: K1, P3, (K3, P3) to last st, K1.
Repeat last 2 rows until scarf measures 16 in. (40 cm) from cast-on edge, ending with a WS row.
Do not bind off. Leave sts on a holder.

Finishing

Slip the first scarf panel onto one needle and the second scarf panel onto another needle. Hold the two panels together with right sides facing each other (wrong sides facing outward), and using a third needle, knit the first st on the front needle together with the first st on the back needle. Do the same for the second sts and then bind off by lifting 1 st over the other. Continue in this way until all sts have been bound off.

tutu

Frilly layers of contrasting textures are used to create this ribbed, easy-to-knit scarf. Tackle one layer at a time and you'll have this sumptous neckwarmer stitched in no time at all!

Materials

Yarn A One 50g ball of Rowan Kid Classic, Color 844 Frilly (used triple)

Yarn B One 100g ball of Rowan Chunky Print, Color 074 Tart

Yarn C Two 100g balls of Rowan Plaid, Color 164 Sea Thistle

US 11 (8 mm) needles

Stitch holder

Spare knitting needle

Gauge

11 sts and 14 rows to 4 in. (10 cm) on US 11 (8 mm) needles measured over stockinette stitch.

Finished Size: 7½ × 72 in. (19 × 180 cm)

Scarf panel (make 2)

First Section

Cast on 81 sts using A (used triple) and US 11 (8 mm) needles.

Row 1: (RS) K1, (K2, lift first of these sts over second) to end. (41 sts)

Row 2: (WS) P1, (P2tog) to end. (21 sts)

Row 3: Knit.

Row 4: K1, (P1, K1) to end.

Repeat last 2 rows 9 more times, ending with a WS row.

Do not bind off. Leave sts on a holder.

Second Section

Cast on 81 sts using B and US 11 (8 mm) needles.

Row 1: (RS) K1, (K2, lift first of these sts over second) to end. (41 sts)

Row 2: (WS) P1, (P2tog) to end. (21 sts)

Next row: Join the second section to the first section as follows: with RS facing, knit together the first st on the needle with the first st on the holder. Continue in this way until the whole row has been completed.

Next row: K1, (P1, K1) to end.

Next row: Knit.

Next row: K1, (P1, K1) to end.

Repeat last 2 rows eight more times, ending with a WS row.

Do not bind off. Leave sts on a holder.

Third Section

Cast on 81 sts using C and US 11 (8 mm) needles.

Row 1: (RS) K1, (K2, lift first of these sts over second) to end. (41 sts)

Row 2: (WS) P1, (P2tog) to end. (21 sts)

Next row: Join the third section to the second section as follows: with RS facing, knit together the first st on the needle with the first st on the holder. Continue in this way until the whole row has been completed.

Next row: K1, (P1, K1) to end.

Next row: Knit.

Next row: K1, (P1, K1) to end.

Repeat last 2 rows until work measures 36 in. (90 cm) from cast-on edge, ending with a WS row.

Do not bind off. Leave sts on a holder.

Finishing

Slip the first scarf panel onto one needle and the second scarf panel onto another needle. Hold the two panels together with right sides facing each other (wrong sides facing outward), and using a third needle, knit the first st on the front needle together with the first st on the back needle. Do the same for the second sts and then bind off by lifting one st over the other. Continue in this way until all sts have been bound off.

swell

Plain and tweed yarn come together to form this quick-stitch bobble hat. A wide ribbed band and a traditional pom-pom on the top finish it off nicely!

Materials

Yarn A One 50g ball of Rowan Wool Cotton, Color 946 Elf *125 yds (DK)*
Yarn B One 50g ball of Rowan Felted Tweed, Color 152 Watery *191 yds (DK)*
US 6 (4 mm) needles
Two circles of cardboard, approx. 1⅜ in. (3.5 cm) in diameter

Gauge

22 sts and 30 rows to 4 in. (10 cm) on US 6 (4 mm) needles measured over stockinette stitch.

Finished size: to fit average-size adult head

Hat

Cast on 104 sts using A and US 6 (4 mm) needles.
Change to B.
Row 1: (RS) K4, (P3, K3) to last 4 sts, P4.
Repeat this row 13 more times, ending with a WS row.
Change to A.
15 **Next row:** Knit, inc 2 sts evenly across this row. (106 sts)
16 **Next row:** Purl.
17 **Next row:** Knit.
**Change to B.
18 **Next row:** Knit. *26, 34*
19 **Next row:** Knit. *27, 35*
20 **Next row:** Purl. *28, 36*
21 **Next row:** Knit. *29, 37*

Change to A.
22 **Next row:** Knit. *30, 38*
23 **Next row:** Knit. *31, 39*
24 **Next row:** Purl. *32, 40*
25 **Next row:** Knit. *33, 41*
Repeat from ** twice more, ending with a RS row.
Change to B.
~~26~~ **Next row:** Knit. *42*
~~27~~ **Next row:** Knit. *43*
~~28~~ **Next row:** Purl. *44*
~~29~~ **Next row:** Knit. *45*
Change to A.
~~30~~ **Next row:** Knit. *46*
~~31~~ **Next row:** Knit. *47*
~~32~~ **Next row:** Purl. *48*
Working in set stripe sequence, shape crown as follows:
~~33~~ **Next row:** (dec row) K1, (K2tog, K5) to end. (91 sts) *49*
~~34~~ **Next row:** Knit. *50*
~~35~~ **Next row:** (dec row) K1, (K2tog, K4) to end. (76 *51* sts)
~~36~~ **Next row:** Purl. *52*
~~37~~ **Next row:** (dec row) K1, (K2tog, K3) to end. (61 sts) *53*
~~38~~ **Next row:** Knit. *54*
~~39~~ **Next row:** (dec row) K1, (K2tog, K2) to end. (46 sts) *55*
~~40~~ **Next row:** Purl. *56*
~~41~~ **Next row:** (dec row) K1, (K2tog, K1) to end. (31 *57* sts)
~~42~~ **Next row:** Knit. *58*
~~43~~ **Next row:** (dec row) K1, (K2tog) to end. (16 sts) *59*
Do not bind off.

Finishing

Thread yarn through remaining sts and pull together. Sew seam starting at the crown and working to the cast-on edge.

Make pom-pom as follows:
Cut a hole in the center of each circle of cardboard approx. ⅝ in. (1.5 cm) in diameter. Hold one strand of A and one strand of B together and wind the yarn through the hole and around the outside of the two circles of cardboard until the center hole is almost filled. Next, cut slowly and carefully around the edges of the two pieces of cardboard until all the yarn has been cut. Carefully ease the pieces of cardboard apart but before taking them off completely, tie a piece of yarn in a secure knot around the center of the pom-pom to hold it together. Now remove the cardboard.
Sew pom-pom to crown of hat.

berry

This beanie-style hat has pretty scalloped edging and bead detail. The rich flecks of color in the tweed adds textural verve to this interesting design.

Materials
Yarn A One 50g ball of Rowan Handknit Cotton, Color 314 Decadent
Yarn B One 50g ball of Rowan Yorkshire Tweed, Color 342 Revel
US 6 (4 mm) needles
Approx. 78 purple beads, 3 mm (J3001014)

Gauge
22 sts and 30 rows to 4 in. (10 cm) on US 6 (4 mm) needles measured over stockinette stitch.

Finished size: to fit average-size adult head.

Abbreviation
PB Place Bead: with yarn in front, slip bead to front of work, sl 1 purlwise, take yarn to back of work. The bead will now be sitting in front of the slipped stitch. See "Knitting with beads" page 80.

Hat
Cast on 106 sts using B and US 6 (4 mm) needles.
Change to A.
Row 1: (RS) K1, (sl 1, K1, psso, K9, K2tog) to last st, K1. (90 sts)
Row 2: (WS) Purl.
Row 3: K1, (sl 1, K1, psso, K7, K2tog) to last st, K1. (74 sts)
Row 4: Purl.
Row 5: K1, *sl 1, K1, psso, YO, (K1, YO) 5 times, K2tog, rep from * to last st, K1. (106 sts)

Row 6: Knit.
Repeat rows 1–6 once more, ending with a WS row.
Change to B.
Row 13: Knit.
Row 14: Purl.
Change to A.
Row 15: Knit.
Row 16: Purl.
Row 17: K1, PB, (K3, PB) to last 4 sts, K4.
Row 18: Purl.
Row 19: (K3, PB) to last 2 sts, K2.
Row 20: Purl.
Row 21: K1, PB, (K3, PB) to last 4 sts, K4.
Row 22: Purl.
Change to B.
Continue in St st until hat measures 7¼ in. (18 cm) from cast-on edge, ending with a WS row.
Next row: (dec row) K1, (K2tog, K5) to end. (91 sts)
Next row: Purl.
Next row: (dec row) K1, (K2tog, K4) to end. (76 sts)
Next row: Purl.
Next row: (dec row) K1, (K2tog, K3) to end. (61 sts)
Next row: Purl.
Next row: (dec row) K1, (K2tog, K2) to end. (46 sts)
Next row: Purl.

Next row: (dec row) K1, (K2tog, K1) to end. (31 sts)
Next row: Purl.
Next row: (dec row) K1, (K2tog) to end. (16 sts)
Do not bind off.

Finishing
Thread yarn through remaining sts and pull together. Sew seam starting at the crown and working to the cast-on edge.

fuchsia

The simplest of beanies, this one can be knitted in next to no time. A single bloom adds a fun youthful touch.

Materials

Yarn A One 50g ball of Rowan Wool Cotton, Color 943 Flower
Yarn B Two 50g balls of Rowan 4 ply Soft, Color 377 Wink (used double)
US 6 (4 mm) needles

Gauge

22 sts and 30 rows to 4 in. (10 cm) using B on US 6 (4 mm) needles measured over stockinette stitch.

Finished size: to fit average-size adult head

Hat

Cast on 106 sts using A and US 6 (4 mm) needles.
Change to B.
Row 1: (RS) (K1, P1) to end.
Row 2: (WS) (P1, K1) to end.
These 2 rows form seed st. Repeat these 2 rows 3 more times, ending with a WS row.
Change to A.
Next row: Knit.
Next row: Purl.
These last 2 rows form St st. Repeat last 2 rows once more.
Change to B.
Continue in St st until hat measures 7¼ in. (18 cm) from cast-on edge, ending with a WS row.
Shape crown as follows:
Next row: (dec row) K1, (K2tog, K5) to end. (91 sts)
Next row: Purl.
Next row: (dec row) K1, (K2tog, K4) to end. (76 sts)
Next row: Purl.
Next row: (dec row) K1, (K2tog, K3) to end.
(61 sts)
Next row: Purl.
Next row: (dec row) K1, (K2tog, K2) to end. (46 sts)
Next row: Purl.
Next row: (dec row) K1, (K2tog, K1) to end. (31 sts)
Next row: Purl.
Next row: (dec row) K1, (K2tog) to end. (16 sts)
Do not bind off. Thread yarn through remaining sts and pull together.

Flower

Cast on 93 sts using A and US 6 (4 mm) needles.
Change to B.
Row 1: K1, (K2, lift first of these sts over second) to end. (47 sts)
Row 2: P1, (P2tog) to end. (24 sts)
Row 3: Knit.
Row 4: Purl.
Do not bind off. Thread yarn through remaining sts and pull together. Twist into flower shape and sew to secure.

Finishing

Sew seam starting at the crown and working toward the cast-on edge. Sew flower into place using the photograph as a guide.

sage

Accessories can be both fun and practical. Flirty frills accent the cuff of these stylish gloves, and tweedy wool yarn will keep your hands toasty all winter long.

Materials

Yarn A One 50g ball of Rowan Felted Tweed, Color 146 Herb

Yarn B One 25g ball of Rowan Kidsilk Haze, Color 597 Jelly (used double)

Yarn C One 50g ball of Rowan Handknit Cotton, Color 219 Gooseberry

US 3 (3.25 mm) needles

US 6 (4 mm) needles

Gauge

22 sts and 30 rows to 4 in. (10 cm) using A on US 6 (4 mm) needles measured over stockinette stitch.

Finished size: to fit average-size adult hand

Right Hand

Cast on 173 sts using B and US 3 (3.25 mm) needles.

Change to C.

Row 1: (RS) K1, (K2, lift first of these sts over second) to end. (87 sts)

Row 2: (WS) P1, (P2tog) to end. (44 sts)

Change to A.

Row 3: (K1, P1) to end.

Repeat this row 23 more times, ending with a WS row.

Change to US 6 (4 mm) needles.

Next row: (inc row) K7, M1, knit to last 7 sts, M1, K7. (46 sts)

Next row: Purl.

Next row: Knit.

Next row: Purl.

*Shape thumb as follows:

Next row: K23, M1, K3, M1, knit to end. (48 sts)

Next row: Purl.

Next row: K23, M1, K5, M1, knit to end. (50 sts)

Next row: Purl.

Next row: K23, M1, K7, M1, knit to end. (52 sts)

Next row: Purl.

Next row: K23, M1, K9, M1, knit to end. (54 sts)

Next row: Purl.

Next row: K23, M1, K11, M1, knit to end. (56 sts)

Next row: Purl.

Next row: K23, M1, K13, M1, knit to end. (58 sts)

Next row: Purl.

Divide for thumb as follows:

Next row: K38, turn.

Next row: P15, turn.

Starting with a knit row, work 14 rows of St st on these 15 sts only, ending with a WS row.

Next row: (K1, K2tog) to end. (10 sts)

Next row: Purl.

Next row: (K2tog) to end. (5 sts)

Break off yarn and thread through remaining 5 sts and pull together.

With RS facing, rejoin yarn at base of thumb to remaining sts and knit to end. (43 sts)

Next row: Purl.

Next row: Knit.

Next row: Purl.

Repeat last 2 rows 4 more times, ending with a WS row.

Work first finger as follows:

Next row: K28, turn.

Next row: P13, turn and cast on 2 sts. (15 sts)

Starting with a knit row, work 18 rows of St st on these 15 sts only, ending with a WS row.

Next row: (K1, K2tog) to end. (10 sts)

Next row: Purl.

Next row: K2tog to end. (5 sts)

Break off yarn and thread through remaining 5 sts and pull together.

Work second finger as follows:

With RS facing, rejoin yarn to remaining sts and pick up 2 sts from base of first finger and K5, turn.

Next row: P12, turn and cast on 2 sts. (14 sts)

Starting with a knit row, work 20 rows of St st on these 14 sts only, ending with a WS row.

Next row: (K1, K2tog) to last 2 sts, K2. (10 sts)

Next row: Purl.

Next row: K2tog to end. (5 sts)

Break off yarn and thread through remaining 5 sts and pull together.

Work third finger as follows:

With RS facing, rejoin yarn to remaining sts and pick up 2 sts from base of second finger and K5, turn.

Next row: P12, turn and cast on 2 sts. (14 sts)
Starting with a knit row, work 18 rows of St st on these 14 sts only, ending with a WS row.

Next row: (K1, K2tog) to last 2 sts, K2. (10 sts)

Next row: Purl.

Next row: (K2tog) to end. (5 sts)
Break off yarn and thread through remaining 5 sts and pull together.

Work fourth finger as follows:

With RS facing, rejoin yarn to remaining sts and pick up 2 sts from base of second finger and K5, turn.

Next row: P12, turn.
Starting with a knit row, work 14 rows of St st, ending with a WS row.

Next row: (K1, K2tog) to end. (8 sts)

Next row: Purl.

Next row: K2tog to end. (4 sts)
Break off yarn and thread through remaining 4 sts and pull together.

Left Hand

Work as for right-hand glove until *.

Shape thumb as follows:

Next row: K20, M1, K3, M1, knit to end. (48 sts)
Next row: Purl.
Next row: K20, M1, K5, M1, knit to end. (50 sts)
Next row: Purl.
Next row: K20, M1, K7, M1, knit to end. (52 sts)
Next row: Purl.
Next row: K20, M1, K9, M1, knit to end. (54 sts)
Next row: Purl.
Next row: K20, M1, K11, M1, knit to end. (56 sts)
Next row: Purl.
Next row: K20, M1, K13, M1, knit to end. (58 sts)
Next row: Purl.
Divide for thumb as follows:
Next row: K35, turn.

Work as for right hand glove from ** to end.

Finishing

Sew thumb and finger seams and side seams.

handy

These cozy fingerless gloves are exactly as their name suggests! A striking contrast is created with the mohair and cotton combination.

Materials

Yarn A One 25g ball of Rowan Kidsilk Haze, Color 600 Dewberry (used double)
Yarn B One 50g ball of Rowan 4 ply Cotton, Color 127 Flirty (used double)
US 3 (3.25 mm) needles
US 6 (4 mm) needles

Gauge

22 sts and 30 rows to 4 in. (10 cm) uisng A on US 6 (4 mm) needles measured over stockinette stitch.

Finished size: to fit average-size adult hand

Right Hand

Cast on 46 sts using A and US 3 (3.25 mm) needles.
Change to B.
Row 1: (RS) (K2, P2) to last 2sts, K2.
Row 2: (WS) (P2, K2) to last 2sts, P2.
Change to A.
Row 3: (K2, P2) to last 2sts, K2.
Row 4: (P2, K2) to last 2sts, P2.
Row 5: (K2, P2) to last 2sts, K2.
Row 6: (P2, K2) to last 2sts, P2.
The last 6 rows form the stripe pattern. Repeat these 6 rows twice more and then repeat rows 1–4 once more.
Change to US 6 (4 mm) needles and B.
Next row: Knit.
Next row: Purl.

Change to A.
Next row: Knit.
Next row: Purl.
Repeat these 2 rows 3 more times.

*Shape thumb as follows:
Next row: K23, M1, K3, M1, knit to end. (48 sts)
Next row: Purl.
Next row: K23, M1, K5, M1, knit to end. (50sts)
Next row: Purl.
Next row: K23, M1, K7, M1, knit to end. (52 sts)
Next row: Purl.
Next row: K23, M1, K9, M1, knit to end. (54 sts)
Next row: Purl.
Next row: K23, M1, K11, M1, knit to end. (56 sts)
Next row: Purl.
Next row: K23, M1, K13, M1, knit to end. (58 sts)
Next row: Purl.

Divide for thumb as follows:
Next row: K38, turn.
****Next row:** P15, turn.
Starting with a knit row, work 6 rows of St st on
these 15 sts only, ending with a WS row.
Change to B.
Bind off loosely.

With RS facing, rejoin yarn A to remaining sts and
knit to end. (43 sts)
Next row: Purl.
Next row: Knit.

Next row: Purl.
Repeat last 2 rows 4 more times, ending with a WS
row.

Work first finger as follows:
Next row: K28, turn.
Next row: P13, turn and cast on 2 sts. (15 sts)
Starting with a knit row, work 6 rows of St st on
these 15 sts only, ending with a WS row.
Change to B.
Bind off loosely.

Work second finger as follows:
With RS facing, rejoin yarn A to remaining sts and
pick up 2 sts from base of first finger and K5, turn.
Next row: P12, turn and cast on 2 sts. (14 sts)
Starting with a knit row, work 6 rows of St st on
these 14 sts only, ending with a WS row.
Change to B.
Bind off loosely.

Work third finger as follows:
With RS facing, rejoin yarn A to remaining sts, pick
up 2 sts from base of second finger and K5, turn.
Next row: P12, turn and cast on 2 sts. (14 sts)
Starting with a knit row, work 6 rows of St st on
these 14 sts only, ending with a WS row.
Change to B.
Bind off loosely.

Work fourth finger as follows:
With RS facing, rejoin yarn A to remaining sts, pick
up 2 sts from base of second finger and K5, turn.
Next row: P12, turn.
Starting with a knit row, work 6 rows of St st,
ending with a WS row.
Change to B.
Bind off loosely.

Left Hand
Work as given for right hand glove until *.
Shape thumb as follows:
Next row: K20, M1, K3, M1, knit to end. (48 sts)
Next row: Purl.
Next row: K20, M1, K5, M1, knit to end. (50 sts)
Next row: Purl.
Next row: K20, M1, K7, M1, knit to end. (52 sts)
Next row: Purl.
Next row: K20, M1, K9, M1, knit to end. (54 sts)
Next row: Purl.
Next row: K20, M1, K11, M1, knit to end. (56 sts)
Next row: Purl.
Next row: K20, M1, K13, M1, knit to end. (58 sts)
Next row: Purl.

Divide for thumb as follows:
Next row: K35, turn.
Work as for right hand glove from ** to end.

Finishing
Sew thumb and finger seams and side seams.

dizzy

Big, bold polka dots are the main act of these winter mittens and this design is spot on. A striking contrast between the colors further accentuates the strong shapes.

Materials

Yarn A One 50g ball of Rowan Kid Classic,
Color 847 Cherry
Yarn B One 50g ball of Rowan Kid Classic,
Color 844 Frilly
US 6 (4 mm) needles
US 7 (4.5 mm) needles

Gauge

20 sts and 26 rows to 4 in. (10 cm) on US 7
(4.5 mm) needles measured over stockinette stitch.

Finished size: to fit average-size adult hand

Right Hand

Cast on 37 sts using B and US 6 (4 mm) needles.
Change to A.
Row 1: (RS) K1, (P1, K1) to end.
Row 2: (WS) P1, (K1, P1) to end.
Repeat last 2 rows 7 more times, ending with a WS row.
Change to B and US 7 (4.5 mm) needles.
Next row: (K6, M1) to last 7 sts, K7. (42 sts)
Next row: Purl.
Next row: Knit.
Next row: Purl.

*Starting with chart row 1 and keeping intarsia pattern correct either side of thumb, shape thumb in B as follows:

Next row: K21, M1, K3, M1, knit to end. (44 sts)
Next row: Purl.
Next row: Knit.
Next row: Purl.
Next row: K21, M1, K5, M1, knit to end. (46 sts)
Next row: Purl.
Next row: K21, M1, K7, M1, knit to end. (48 sts)
Next row: Purl.
Next row: K21, M1, K9, M1, knit to end. (50 sts)
Next row: Purl.
Next row: K21, M1, K11, M1, knit to end. (52 sts)
Next row: Purl.

Divide for thumb as follows:
Next row: K34, turn.
**Using only B, work thumb as follows:
Next row: P13, turn.
Starting with a knit row, work 10 rows of St st on these 13 sts only, ending with a WS row.
Next row: K1 (K2tog) to end. (7 sts)
Break off yarn and thread through remaining 7 sts and pull together.
Rejoin yarn at base of thumb and keeping chart pattern correct, inc 3 sts (2A, 1B) and work to end. (42 sts)

Yarn A
Yarn B

Starting with chart row 14, continue without shaping following chart until chart row 30 has been completed.

Using only B and no longer working from chart, shape top as follows:

Next row: K4, K3tog, (K7, K3tog) to last 5 sts, K5. (34 sts)

Next row: Purl.

Next row: Knit.

Next row: Purl.

Next row: K3, K3tog, (K5, K3tog) to last 4 sts, K4. (26 sts)

Next row: Purl.

Next row: Knit.

Next row: Purl.

Next row: K2, K3tog (K3, K3tog) to last 3 sts, K3. (18 sts)

Next row: Purl.

Bind off.

Left Hand

Work as given for right-hand mitten until *.

Next row: K18, M1, K3, M1, knit to end. (44 sts)

Next row: Purl.

Next row: Knit.

Next row: Purl.

Next row: K18, M1, K5, M1, knit to end. (46 sts)

Next row: Purl.

Next row: K18, M1, K7, M1, knit to end. (48 sts)

Next row: Purl.

Next row: K18, M1, K9, M1, knit to end. (50 sts)

Next row: Purl.

Next row: K18, M1, K11, M1, knit to end. (52 sts)

Next row: Purl.

Divide for thumb as follows:

Next row: K31, turn.

Now work as for right-hand mitten from ** to end, working inc 3 sts at base of thumb as 3A, instead of 2A, 1B.

Finishing

Sew side seams, starting at the cast-on edge and working up the side and across the top.

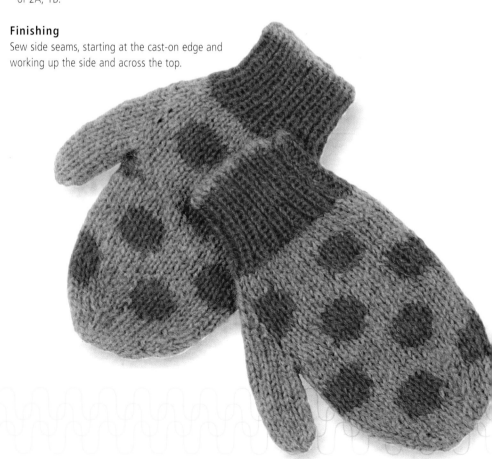

snug

These very simple-to-knit hand warmers are a great alternative to gloves. The combination of cotton, tweed, and mohair is complemented with a matching button.

Materials

Yarn A One 50g ball of Rowan Felted Tweed,
 Color 154 Ginger
Yarn B One 50g ball of Rowan Glace,
 Color 739 Dijon
Yarn C One 25g ball of Rowan Kidsilk Haze,
 Color 596 Marmalade (used double)
US 3 (3.25 mm) needles
US 5 (3.75 mm) needles
Two orange buttons (Rowan 00372), 2 cm
 diameter

Gauge

24 sts and 32 rows to 4 in. (10 cm) using yarn A on US 3 (3.25 mm) needles measured over stockinette stitch.

Finished size: to fit average-size adult hand

Right Hand

Cast on 46 sts using C and US 5 (3.75 mm)
 needles.
Row 1 rib pattern: (RS) K2, (P2, K2) to end.
Row 2 rib pattern: (WS) P2, (K2, P2) to end.
Starting with a RS row, continue in rib pattern as
 set, working stripes as follows:
1 row in B.
9 rows in A.
1 row in C.
1 row in B.
1 row in C.

9 rows in A.
1 row in C.
1 row in B.
1 row in A.
1 row in C.
1 row in B.
1 row in A.
1 row in C.
1 row in B.
1 row in A.
3 rows in B.
Rest of hand warmer is now worked in St st.
Change to A and US 3 (3.25 mm) needles.
Next row: Knit.
Next row: Purl*.
Shape thumb as follows:
Next row: K23, M1, K3, M1, knit to end. (48 sts)
Next row: Purl.
Next row: K23, M1, K5, M1, knit to end. (50 sts)
Next row: Purl.
Next row: K23, M1, K7, M1, knit to end. (52 sts)
Next row: Purl.
Next row: K23, M1, K9, M1, knit to end. (54 sts)
Next row: Purl.
Next row: K23, M1, K11, M1, knit to end. (56 sts)
Next row: Purl.
Next row: K23, M1, K13, M1, knit to end. (58 sts)
Next row: Purl.

Divide for thumb as follows:
Next row: K38, turn.
**Next row: P15, turn.
Starting with a knit row, work 6 rows of St st on
these 15 sts only, ending with a WS row.
Bind off.

With RS facing, rejoin A at base of thumb to
remaining sts and knit to end. (43 sts)
Next row: Purl.
Next row: Knit.
Next row: Purl.
Repeat last 2 rows twice more, ending with a WS
row.
Change to C.
Next row: Knit.
Next row: Purl.
Next row: Knit.
Repeat last 2 rows twice more, ending with a RS
row.
Next row: Knit. (This creates garter stitch ridge for
turn over at top.)
Next row: Knit.
Next row: Purl.
Next row: Knit.
Next row: Purl.
Bind off loosely.

Left Hand
Work as for right hand until *.
Shape thumb as follows:
Next row: K20, M1, K3, M1, knit to end. (48 sts)
Next row: Purl.
Next row: K20, M1, K5, M1, knit to end. (50 sts)
Next row: Purl.
Next row: K20, M1, K7, M1, knit to end. (52 sts)
Next row: Purl.
Next row: K20, M1, K9, M1, knit to end. (54 sts)
Next row: Purl.
Next row: K20, M1, K11, M1, knit to end. (56 sts)
Next row: Purl.
Next row: K20, M1, K13, M1, knit to end. (58 sts)
Next row: Purl.

Divide for thumb as follows:
Next row: K35, turn.
Work as for right hand from ** to end.

Finishing
Turn under the top of each hand warmer along the
garter stitch ridge and slip stitch into place using C.
Sew thumb and side seams. Sew one decorative
button to each cuff.

cozy toes

These ultra-comfy socks will keep your toes warm on the coldest of winter days. A medley of vibrant colors and mohair, wool, and tweed textures have been used to create a cheerful, striped pattern.

Materials

Yarn A Two 50g balls of Rowan 4 ply Soft, Color 370 Whisper

Yarn B One 50g ball of Rowan 4 ply Soft, Color 377 Wink

Yarn C One 25g ball of Rowan Kidsilk Haze, Color 597 Jelly

Yarn D One 25g ball of Rowan Kidsilk Haze, Color 606 Candy Girl

Yarn E One 25g ball of Rowan Kidsilk Haze, Color 582 Trance

Yarn F One 25g ball of Rowan Yorkshire Tweed 4 ply, Color 271 Cheerful

Yarn G One 25g ball of Rowan Yorkshire Tweed 4 ply, Color 272 Butterscotch

Yarn H One 50g ball of Rowan 4 ply Soft, Color 379 Goblin

US 3 (3 mm) needles
US 3 (3.25 mm) needles
Stitch holder
Spare knitting needle

Gauge

28 sts and 36 rows to 4 in. (10 cm) on US 3 (3.25 mm) needles measured over stockinette stitch.

Finished size: to fit average-size adult foot

Sock (make 2)

Cast on 65 sts using E and US 3 (3.25 mm) needles.
Change to A and US 2 or 3 (3mm) needles.
Row 1: (RS) K1, (P1, K1) to end.
Row 2: (WS) P1, (K1, p1) to end.
Rep last 2 rows 7 more times, ending with a WS row.
Change to US 3 (3.25 mm) needles.
Starting with a knit row, continue in St st working stripes as follows:

2 rows in H.
1 row in C.
1 row in B.
1 row in D.
1 row in F.
1 row in E.
3 rows in A.
2 rows in H.
2 rows in C.
2 rows in G.
4 rows in B.
4 rows in E.
2 rows in F.
2 rows in A.
6 rows in C.
4 rows in D.
2 rows in B.
6 rows in F.
2 rows in A.
10 rows in H.
10 rows in D.
10 rows in E.
2 rows in A.
10 rows in G.
10 rows in B, ending with a WS row.
Rest of sock is now worked in A only.
Next row: Knit.
Break off yarn.

Shape heel

Slip first 15 sts onto right needle, slip middle 34 instep sts onto a holder, and slip last 16 sts onto a spare needle.
With RS facing, rejoin yarn to instep edge of the 15 sts.
Next row: K14, knit tog next st with first st on spare needle, knit to end. (30 sts)
Next row: Purl.
Next row: Knit.
Rep last 2 rows 7 more times, ending with a RS row.
Next row: Purl.

Turn Heel

K17, K2tog, K1, turn.
P5, P2tog, P1, turn.
K6, K2tog, K1, turn.
P7, P2tog, P1, turn.
K8, K2tog, K1, turn.
P9, P2tog, P1, turn.
K10, K2tog, K1, turn.

P11, P2tog, P1, turn.
K12, K2tog, K1, turn.
P13, P2tog, P1, turn.
K14, K2tog, K1, turn.
P15, P2tog, P2, turn. (18 sts)
Break off yarn.

With RS facing, rejoin yarn and pick up and knit 11 sts down one side of heel, knit 18 sts across heel, and pick up and knit 11 sts up the other side of heel. (40 sts)

Next row: Purl.

Next row: Knit.

Next row: Purl.

Rep last 2 rows once more, ending with WS row.

Next: K1, K2tog tbl, knit to last 3 sts, K2tog, K1. (38 sts)

Next row: Purl.

Next row: Knit.

Next row: Purl.

Next row: K1, K2tog tbl, knit to last 3 sts, K2tog, K1. (36 sts)

Rep last 4 rows twice more, ending with a RS row. (32 sts)

Starting with a purl row, continue in St st until sole measures 8 in. (20 cm) from back of heel, ending with a WS row.

Shape toe

Next row: K1, K2tog tbl, knit to last 3sts, K2tog, K1. (30sts)

Next row: Purl.

Next row: K1, K2tog tbl, knit to last 3 sts, K2tog, K1. (28 sts)

Rep last 2 rows twice more, ending with a RS row. (24 sts)

Next row: Purl.

Next row: K1, K2tog tbl, knit to last 3 sts, K2tog, K1. (22 sts)

Next row: P1, P2tog, purl to last 3 sts, P2tog tbl, P1. (20 sts)

Rep last 2 rows until 12 sts remain, ending with a WS row.

Bind off.

Instep

With RS facing, rejoin yarn to 34 sts on holder.

Next row: Knit.

Next row: Purl.

Rep last 2 rows until instep is the same length as sole to toe shaping, ending with a WS row.

Shape toe

Next row: K1, K2tog tbl, knit to last 3 sts, K2tog, K1. (32 sts)

Next row: Purl.

Next row: K1, K2tog tbl, knit to last 3 sts, K2tog, K1. (30 sts)

Rep last 2 rows 3 more times, ending with a RS row. (24 sts)

Next row: Purl

Next row: K1, K2tog tbl, knit to last 3 sts, K2tog, K1. (22 sts)

Next row: P1, P2tog, purl to last 3 sts, P2tog tbl, P1. (20 sts)

Rep last 2 rows until 12 sts remain, ending with a WS row.

Bind off.

Finishing

Join leg seam. Join instep to sole by working along one side of foot, across the toe and along the other side of foot.

rhubarb

The softest of yarns provide added comfort to these extra-snug ankle-length socks. The pretty picot edging lends a subtle feminine touch.

Materials
Yarn A One 50g ball of Rowan Calmer,
  Color 474 Khaki
Yarn B One 50g ball of Rowan Calmer,
  Color 477 Blush
US 6 (4 mm) needles
US 7 (4.5 mm) needles
Stitch holder
Spare knitting needle

Gauge
21 sts and 30 rows to 4 in. (10 cm) on US 7 (4.5 mm) needles measured over stockinette stitch.

Finished size: to fit average-size adult foot

Sock (make 2)
Cast on using A and US 6 (4 mm) needles as
  follows:
(Cast on 7 sts, bind off 3 sts, sl st on right needle
  back on to the left needle) 11 times, cast on
  2 sts. (46 sts)
Change to B.
Row 1: (RS) (K1, P1) to end.
Repeat this row 7 more times, ending with
  a WS row.
Change to US 7 (4.5 mm) needles.
Next row: Knit.
Next row: Purl.
Repeat last 2 rows 3 more times, ending with
  a WS row.

Next row: Knit.
Break off yarn.

Shape heel

Slip first 11 sts onto right needle, slip middle 23 instep sts onto a holder and slip last 12 sts onto a spare needle.

With RS facing, rejoin A to instep edge of the 11 sts.

Next row: K10, knit tog next st with first st on spare needle, knit to end. (22 sts)

Next row: Purl.

Next row: Knit.

Repeat last 2 rows 6 more times, ending with a RS row.

Next row: Purl.

Turn Heel

K13, K2tog, K1, turn.
P5, P2tog, P1, turn.
K6, K2tog, K1, turn.
P7, P2tog, P1, turn.
K8, K2tog, K1, turn.
P9, P2tog, P1, turn.
K10, K2tog, K1, turn.
P11, P2tog, P2. (14 sts)
Break off yarn.

With RS facing, rejoin B and pick up and K9 sts down one side of heel, K14 sts across heel and pick up and K9 sts up the other side of heel. (32 sts)

Next row: Purl.
Next row: Knit.
Next row: Purl.
Next row: K1, K2tog tbl, knit to last 3 sts, K2tog, K1. (30 sts)
Next row: Purl.
Next row: K1, K2tog tbl, knit to last 3 sts, K2tog, K1. (28 sts)
Repeat last 2 rows twice more, ending with a RS row. (24 sts)
Starting with a purl row, continue in St st until sole measures 8 in. (20 cm) from back of heel, ending with a WS row.
Change to A.

Shape toe

Next row: K1, K2tog tbl, knit to last 3 sts, K2tog, K1. (22 sts)
Next row: Purl.
Next row: K1, K2tog tbl, knit to last 3 sts, K2tog, K1. (20 sts)
Rep last 2 rows 3 more times, ending with a RS row. (14 sts)
Next row: P1, P2tog, purl to last 3 sts, P2tog tbl, P1. (12sts)
Bind off.

Instep

With RS facing, rejoin B to 23 sts on holder.
Next row: Knit.
Next row: Purl.

Repeat last 2 rows until instep is the same length as sole to toe shaping, ending with a WS row.
Change to A.

Shape toe

Next row: K1, K2tog tbl, knit to last 3 sts, K2tog, K1. (21 sts)
Next row: Purl.
Next row: K1, K2tog tbl, knit to last 3 sts, K2tog, K1. (19 sts)
Repeat last 2 rows 3 more times, ending with a RS row. (13 sts)
Next row: P1, P2tog, purl to last 3 sts, P2tog tbl, P1. (11 sts)
Bind off.

Finishing

Join leg seam. Join instep to sole by working along one side of foot, across the toe and along the other side of foot.

black currant

Looking for a quick knitting fix? Knit with big needles in chunky yarn and this belt is guaranteed to stitch up in a flash! Delicate flowers have been embroidered in a fine cotton and enhanced with a cluster of beads in the center.

Materials

Yarn A One 100g ball of Rowan Big Wool, Color 025 Wild Berry
Yarn B One 50g ball of Rowan 4 ply Cotton, Color 130 Ardour
US 17 (12 mm) needles
Approx. 36 mauve beads, 3 mm (J3001020)
Medium crochet hook

Gauge

8 sts and 12 rows to 4 in. (10 cm) using A on US 17 (12 mm) needles measured over stockinette stitch.

Finished size: 2½ × 31 in. (6 × 78 cm)

Belt

Cast on 5 sts using A and US 17 (12 mm) needles.
Row 1: (RS) (K1, P1) to last st, K1.
This row forms the seed st pattern. Repeat this row 9 more times, ending with a WS row.
Row 11: Knit.
Row 12: K1, P3, K1.
Repeat last 2 rows 4 more times, ending with a WS row.
Rows 21–26: Work as row 1.

Repeat rows 11–20 once more, ending with a WS row.
Continue in seed st as set by row 1 until work measures 19 in. (47 cm) from cast-on edge, ending with a WS row.
Repeat rows 11–26 once and then repeat rows 11–20 once more, ending with a WS row.
Next row: Work as row 1.
Repeat this row 9 more times, ending with a WS row.
Bind off.

Finishing

Using the photograph as a guide, and using B, embroider three daisies (see p.79) onto each of the St st panels. You will have 12 daisies in total. See "Lazy daisy" sritch on page 79. Sew three beads into each of the flower centers.

Tassels (make 10)

Cut ten 24 in. (60 cm) lengths of B.
Fold one strand in half, and using a medium crochet hook, thread the folded loop through the corner of the cast-on edge, then fold the ends back through the loop and pull to secure. Do the same at the other corner of the cast-on edge. Attach three more tassels spread evenly in between. Tie all five tassels in a knot at the end. Attach five tassels to the bound-off edge in the same way.

praline

This wide belt is all about texture. Lurex Shimmer loops create a fun three-dimensional knit, and a chunky buckle is used for the fastening.

Materials

Yarn A One 50g ball of Rowan Calmer, Color 481 Coffee Bean

Yarn B One 25g ball of Rowan Lurex Shimmer, Color 335 Bronze

Yarn C One 25g ball of Rowan Lurex Shimmer, Color 330 Copper

US 7 (4.5 mm) needles

One brown buckle (Rowan Z075-366), 1½ x 2 in. (4 x 6 cm)

Lining fabric, approx. 8 × 32 in. (20 × 80 cm)

Gauge

21 sts and 30 rows to 4 in. (10 cm) using A on US 7 (4.5 mm) needles measured over stockinette stitch.

Finished size: 4 × 35 in. (10 × 88 cm)

Abbreviation

ML Make Loop: Knit into next st and before slipping the st off the left needle, bring yarn to the front of the work between the needle points and wrap around your thumb to create loop and then back through the needle points. Now, knit into the st again and then slip off needle. You will now have two sts on the right hand needle. Bind off one by lifting the first stitch over the second. Make sure that when working rows with loops, alternate between B and C. Use C for loops on the first loop row, B for loops on the second loop row, C for loops on the third loop row, and so on.

Belt

Cast on 11 sts using A and on US 7 (4.5 mm) needles.

Row 1: (RS) Knit.

Row 2: (WS) Purl.

Repeat last 2 rows 3 more times, ending with a WS row.

Row 9: Knit.

Row 10: Knit. (This creates garter stitch ridge for turn over hem.)

Row 11: Knit.

Row 12: Purl.

Repeat last 2 rows until work measures 4¾ in. (12 cm) from garter stitch ridge, ending with a WS row.

Next row: K1, M1, knit to last st, M1, K1. (13 sts)

Next row: Purl.

Next row: K1, M1, ML, (K1, ML) to last st, M1, K1. (15 sts)

Repeat last 2 rows until 23 sts, alternating between B and C for loops as described, ending with a WS row.

Next row: K1, ML, (K1, ML) to last st, K1.

Next row: Purl.

Next row: K2, ML, (K1, ML) to last 2sts, K2.

Next row: Purl.

Repeat last 4 rows until work measures 32 in. (80 cm) from cast-on edge, ending with a WS row.

Next row: K2tog, (K1, ML) to last 3 sts, K1, K2tog. (21 sts)

Next row: Purl.

Repeat last 2 rows 3 more times, ending with a WS row. (15 sts)

Next row: K2tog, knit to last 2 sts, K2tog. (13 sts)

Next row: Purl.

Next row: K2tog, knit to last 2 sts, K2tog. (11 sts)

Next row: Purl.

Next row: Knit.

Repeat last 2 rows until work measures 3¼ in. (8 cm) from end of loop pattern, ending with a RS row.

Next row: Knit. (This creates garter stitch ridge for turn over hem.)

Next row: Knit.

Next row: Purl.

Repeat last 2 rows 3 more times, ending with a WS row.

Bind off.

Finishing

Make fabric lining as follows:

Using the looped area of the belt as a template, cut a piece of lining fabric allowing an extra ⅜ in. (1 cm) all a round. Sew a ⅜ in. (1 cm) hem all around, as the edges will be seen. Slip stitch the fabric to the back of the belt.

Thread the bound-off edge of the belt around the middle of the buckle, fold the garter stitch ridge over and slip stitch in place. Fold the other end of belt at the garter stitch ridge onto the WS, and slip stitch in place.

COCO

Put your best foot forward—a pair of leg warmers will keep you warm on those chilly mornings. Thick and thin stripes, highlighted with hints of shimmering Lurex, create a look that's fun and youthful.

Materials
Yarn A One 50g ball of Rowan Calmer, Color 480 Peacock
Yarn B One 50g ball of Rowan Calmer, Color 463 Calmer
Yarn C One 50g ball of Rowan Calmer, Color 474 Khaki
Yarn D One 25g ball of Rowan Lurex Shimmer, Color 333 Pewter (used double throughout)
US 6 (4 mm) needles
US 8 (5 mm) needles

Gauge
19 sts and 27 rows to 4 in. (10 cm) using A on US 8 (5 mm) needles measured over stockinette stitch.

Finished size: 6¼ × 13 in. (15.75 × 33 cm)

Legwarmer (make 2)
Cast on 56 sts using A and US 6 (4 mm) needles.
Change to B.
Row 1: (K1, P1) to end.
Repeat last row 11 more times, ending wth a WS row.
Change to C and US 8 (5 mm) needles.
Row 13: K7, M1, (K14, M1) to last 7 sts, K7. (60 sts)
Row 14: Purl.

Starting with a knit row, continue in St st working stripes as follows:
1 row in D.
2 rows in A.
11 rows in B.
2 rows in A.
1 row in D.
2 rows in B.
11 rows in C.
2 rows in B.
1 row in D.
2 rows in C.
11 rows in A.
2 rows in C.
1 row in D.
2 rows in A.
11 rows in B.
2 rows in A.
1 row in D.
2 rows in C, ending with a RS row.
Change to B.
Next row: P6, P2tog, P13, (P2tog, P13) to last 9 sts, P2tog, P7. (56 sts)
Change to US 6 (4 mm) needles.
Next row: (K1, P1) to end.
Repeat last row 10 more times, ending with a RS row.

Change to A.
Next row: (K1, P1) to end.
Bind off in pattern.

Finishing
Sew side seams.

lottie

Your feet will be lovely and oh-so-snug in these toasty slippers! Wear them plain or finish them off with a complementary bloom.

Materials

Yarn A Two 50g balls of Rowan Handknit Cotton, Color 309 Celery

Yarn B One 50g ball of Rowan Kid Classic, Color 845 Battle

US 6 (4 mm) needles

US 3 (3.25 mm) needles

US 7 (4.5 mm) crochet hook

Gauge

20 sts and 32 rows to 4 in. (10 cm) using B on US 6 (4 mm) needles measured over stockinette stitch.

Finished size: to fit average-size adult foot (length can be altered if desired)

First section (make 2)

Cast on 12 sts in A and 15 sts in B using US 6 (4 mm) needles. (27 sts)

Row 1: Using B, K15, using A, sl 1 st purlwise, (K1, P1) to last st, K1.

Row 2: Using A, (K1, P1) 6 times, using B, P15.

Repeat last 2 rows until work measures 5½ in. (14 cm), ending with a WS row.

> ### note
> Slipper size can be made smaller or bigger by adjusting the length here.

Next row: (dec) Using B, K2tog, K13, using A, sl 1 st purlwise, K1 (P1, K1) to last 2 sts, K2tog. (25 sts)

Next row: Using A, (P1, K1) 5 times, P1, using B, purl to end.

Next row: Using B, K14, using A, sl 1 st purlwise, (K1, P1) to end.

Next row: Using A, (P1, K1) 5 times, P1, using B, purl to end.

Next row: (dec) Using B, K2tog, K12, using A, sl 1 st purlwise, (K1, P1) to last 2 sts, K2tog. (23 sts)

Next row: Using A, (K1, P1) 5 times, using B, purl to end.

Next row: Using B, K13, using A, sl 1 st purlwise, (K1, P1) to last st, K1.

Next row: Using A, (K1, P1) 5 times, using B, purl to end.

Next row: (dec) Using B, K2tog, K11, using A, sl 1 st purlwise, (K1, P1) 3 times, K1, K2tog. (21 sts)

Next row: Using A, (P1, K1) 4 times, P1, using B, purl to end.

Next row: Using B, K12, using A, sl 1 st purlwise, (K1, P1) to end.

Next row: Using A, (P1, K1) 4 times, P1, using B, purl to end.

Next row: (dec) Using B, K2tog, K10, using A, sl 1 st purlwise, (K1, P1) 3 times, K2tog. (19 sts)

Next row: Using A, (K1, P1) 4 times, using B, purl to end.

Next row: (dec) Using B, K2tog, K9, using A, sl 1 st purlwise, (K1, P1) to last 3 sts, K1, K2tog. (17 sts)

Next row: Using A, (P1, K1) 3 times, P1, using B, purl to end.

Next row: (dec) Using B, K2tog, K8, using A, sl 1 st purlwise, (K1, P1) to last 2 sts, K2tog. (15 sts)

Next row: Using A, (K1, P1) 3 times, using B, purl to end.

Next row: (dec) Using B, K2tog, K7, using A, sl 1 st purlwise, K1, P1, K1, K2tog. (13 sts)

Next row: Using A, (P1, K1) twice, P1, using B, purl to end.

Next row: (dec) Using B, K2tog, K6, using A, sl 1 st purlwise, K1, P1 , K2tog. (11 sts)

Next row: Using A, (K1, P1) twice, using B, purl to end.

Next row: (dec) Using B, K2tog, K5, using A, sl 1 st purlwise, K1, K2tog. (9 sts)

Next row: (dec) Using A, K2tog, P1, using B, P3tog, P1, P2tog. (5 sts)

Bind off.

Second section (make 2)

Cast on 15 sts in B and 12 sts in A using US 6 (4 mm) needles. (27 sts)

Row 1: Using A, (K1, P1) 5 times, K1, sl 1 st purlwise, using B, K15.

Row 2: Using B, P15, using A, P1 (K1, P1) 5 times, K1.

Repeat last 2 rows until work measures 5½ in. (14 cm), ending with a WS row.

Next row: (dec) Using A, K2tog, (K1, P1) 4 times, K1, sl 1 st purlwise, using B, knit to last 2 sts, K2tog. (25 sts)

Next row: Using B, P14, using A, (P1, K1) 5 times, P1.

Next row: Using A, (P1, K1) 5 times, sl 1 st purlwise, using B, knit to end.

Next row: Using B, P14, using A, (P1, K1) 5 times, P1.

Next row: (dec) Using A, K2tog, (P1, K1) 4 times, sl 1 st purlwise, using B, knit to last 2 sts, K2tog. (23 sts)

Next row: Using B, P13, using A, (P1, K1) to end.

Next row: Using A, (K1, P1) 4 times, K1, sl 1 st purlwise, using B, knit to end.

Next row: Using B, P13, using A, (P1, K1) to end.

Next row: (dec) Using A, K2tog, (K1, P1) 3 times, K1, sl 1 st purlwise, using B, knit to last 2 sts, K2tog. (21 sts)

Next row: Using B, P12, using A, (P1, K1) 4 times, P1.

Next row: Using A, (P1, K1) 4 times, sl 1 st purlwise, using B, knit to end.

Next row: Using B, P12, using A, (P1, K1) 4 times, P1.

Next row: (dec) Using A, K2tog, (P1, K1) 3 times, sl 1 st purlwise, using B, knit to last 2 sts, K2tog. (19 sts)

Next row: Using B, P11, using A, (P1, K1) to end.

Next row: (dec) Using A, K2tog, (K1, P1) twice, K1, sl 1 st purlwise, using B, knit to last 2 sts, K2tog. (17 sts)

Next row: Using B, P10, using A, (P1, K1) 3 times, P1.

Next row: (dec) Using A, K2tog, (P1, K1) twice, sl 1 st purlwise, using B, knit to last 2 sts, K2tog. (15 sts)

Next row: Using B, P9, using A, (P1, K1) to end.

Next row: (dec) Using A, K2tog, K1, P1, K1, sl 1 st purlwise, using B, knit to last 2 sts, K2tog. (13 sts)

Next row: Using B, P8, using A, (P1, K1) twice, P1.

Next row: (dec) Using A, K2tog, P1, K1, sl 1 st purlwise, using B, knit to last 2 sts, K2tog. (11 sts)

Next row: Using B, P7, using A, (P1, K1) to end.

Next row: (dec) Using A, K2tog, K1, sl 1 st purlwise, using B, knit to last 2 sts, K2tog. (9 sts)

Next row: (dec) Using B, P2tog, P1, P3tog, using A, P1, K2tog. (5 sts)

Bind off.

Heel (make 2)

Cast on 24 sts using A and US 6 (4 mm) needles.

Row 1: (K1, P1) to end.

Row 2: (P1, K1) to end.

These 2 rows form seed st.

Continue in seed st, dec one st at each end of every following row, until 4 sts remain.

Work two more rows of seed st without shaping. Bind off.

Flower (make 2)

Cast on 93 sts using A and US 3 (3.25 mm) needles.

Row 1: K1, (K2, lift first of these sts over second) to end. (47 sts)

Row 2: P1, (P2tog) to end. (24 sts)

Change to B.

Row 3: Knit.

Row 4: Purl.

Do not bind off. Thread yarn through rem 24 sts and pull together.

Finishing

Join the seed stitch panel of the first section to the seed stitch panel of the second to make the sole. Starting at the toe, sew a 6 in. (15 cm) seam up the center of the upper half of the slipper, leaving a gap for the foot to fit through. Sew the cast-on edge of the heel to the cast-on edges of the sole, then sew the side seams of the heel to the back edges of the St st panels.

Using A and US 7 (4.5 mm) crochet hook, start at the center back and work 18 treble crochets down one side of foot opening and then 18 treble crochets up the other side.

Using the photograph on page 74 as a guide, sew the flowers into place.

joy

We all need somewhere to keep our ever-expanding collection of knitting needles and this needle holder should solve the problem! Each pocket is knitted using a different technique so it's a great opportunity to try out something new.

Materials

Yarn A Four 50g skeins of Rowan Summer Tweed, Color 512 Exotic

Yarn B Four 50g balls of Rowan All Seasons Cotton, Color 192 Iceberg

Yarn C One 50g ball of Rowan Wool Cotton, Color 959 Bilberry Fool

Yarn D One 50g ball of Rowan Handknit Cotton, Color 303 Sugar

Yarn E One 50g ball of Rowan Cotton Glace, Color 814 Shoot

Yarn F One 50g ball of Rowan 4 ply Cotton, Color 129 Aegean

Yarn G One 50g ball of Rowan 4 ply Soft, Color 370 Whisper

Yarn H One 50g ball of Rowan Kid Classic, Color 835 Royal

US 3 (3.25 mm) needles

US 6 (4 mm) needles

US 7 (4.5 mm) needles

US 8 (5 mm) needles

Cable needle

Approx. 60 green beads, 3 mm (J3001022)

80 in. (200 cm) length of ½ in. (15 mm) wide turquoise ribbon

Sewing needle and turquoise thread

Gauge

Summer Tweed: 16 sts and 23 rows to 4 in. (10 cm) on US 8 (5 mm) needles measured over stockinette stitch.

All Seasons Cotton: 18 sts and 25 rows to 4 in. (10 cm) on US 7 (4.5 mm) needles measured over stockinette stitch.

Wool Cotton: 22 sts and 30 rows to 4 in. (10 cm) on US 6 (4 mm) needles measured over stockinette stitch.

Handknit Cotton: 20 sts and 28 rows to 4 in. (10 cm) on US 6 (4 mm) needles measured over stockinette stitch.

Cotton Glace: 23 sts and 32 rows to 4 in. (10 cm) on US 3 (3.25 mm) needles measured over stockinette stitch.

4ply Cotton: 28 sts and 36 rows to 4 in. (10 cm) on US 3 (3.25 mm) needles measured over stockinette stitch.

4ply Soft: 28 sts and 36 rows to 4 in. (10 cm) on US 3 (3.25 mm) needles measured over stockinette stitch.

Kid Classic: 19 sts and 25 rows to 4 in. (10 cm) on US 8 (5 mm) needles measured over stockinette stitch.

Finished size: 25 × 21 in. (63 × 53 cm)

Abbreviations

PB Place Bead: WYIF, slip bead to front of work, sl 1 st purlwise, take yarn to back of work. The bead will now be sitting in front of the slipped stitch.

C6B Cable 6 Back: Slip next 4 sts onto cable needle and hold at back of work, K2 sts from left-hand needle, then K4 sts from cable needle.

Outer section

Cast on 85 sts using A and US 8 (5 mm) needles.

Row 1: (RS) Knit.

Row 2: (WS) Purl.

Repeat these last 2 rows once more.

Row 5: Knit.

Next row: Knit. (This creates garter stitch ridge for turn over hem.)

Work 4 more rows even, ending with WS row.

Next row: Cast on 4 sts at beg of next 2 rows. (93 sts)

Next row: K4, sl 1, knit to last 5 sts, sl 1, K4.

Next row: Purl.

---

note

These last two rows set the stockinette stitch pattern with fifth st in from each end worked as a slipped stitch to create a turn under ridge for hem.

Repeat these last 2 rows, keeping in pattern, until 25 in. (63 cm) from cast-on edge, ending with a RS row.

Next row: Bind off 4 sts at beg of next 2 rows. (85 sts)

Next row: Purl.

Next row: Knit.

Next row: Purl.

Next row: Knit.

Next row: Knit. (This creates garter stitch ridge for turn over hem.)

Work 6 more rows even, ending with WS row. Bind off.

Inner section

Cast on 95 sts using B and US 7 (4.5 mm) needles.

Row 1: (RS) Knit.

Row 2: (WS) Purl.

These last 2 rows form St st. Repeat these 2 rows until work measures 25 in. (63 cm) from cast-on edge, ending with a WS row.

Bind off.

Embroidered pocket

Cast on 26 sts using C and US 6 (4 mm) needles.

Row 1: (RS) Knit.

Row 2: (WS) Purl.

Repeat last 2 rows until pocket measures 8½ in. (21 cm), ending with a RS row.

Next row: Knit. (This creates garter stitch ridge for turn over at top of pocket.)

Next row: Knit.

Next row: Purl.

Next row: Knit.

Next row: Purl.

Bind off.

Finishing

Using the photograph as a guide and D, embroider 8 lazy daisies onto pocket.

Lazy daisy stitch

This is a method of working individual chain stitches, which are fastened with a small tying stitch, to form "petals" which can be grouped together to make a "flower" of 4, 5, or more petals.

Knitting with beads

1 Fold a length of embroidery floss in half and thread both ends through a sewing needle. Thread the end of the yarn through the loop in the floss and fold it back on itself. Thread beads along the needle, down the floss and onto the yarn until you have the number of beads on the yarn that your pattern requires.

2 On a right side row, knit to the position of the beaded stitch. Bring the yarn forward to the front of the work and push a bead down the yarn close to the last stitch so that it lies over the front of the next stitch.

3 Slip the next stitch purlwise, leaving the bead in front of the slipped stitch. Take the yarn to the back and continue the work as normal.

Beaded pocket

Cast on 19 sts using E and US 3 (3.25 mm) needles.

Row 1: (RS) Knit.
Row 2: (WS) Purl.
Row 3: (K3, PB) to last 3 sts, K3.
Row 4: Purl.
Row 5: Knit.
Row 6: Purl.
Row 7: K5 (PB, K3) to last 6 sts, PB, K5.
Row 8: Purl.
Row 9: Knit.
Row 10: Purl.
Repeat rows 3–10 seven more times, ending with a WS row.
Next row: Work as row 3.
Next row: Purl.
Next row: Knit.

Next row: Knit. (This creates garter stitch ridge for turn over at top of pocket.)
Next row: Knit.
Next row: Purl.
Next row: Knit.
Next row: Purl.
Bind off.

Cabled pocket

Cast on 16 sts using D and US 6 (4 mm) needles.
Row 1: (RS) (K1, P1) twice, K8, (P1, K1) to end.
Row 2: (WS) K1, (P1, K1) twice, P6, K1, (P1, K1) to end.
Repeat last 2 rows once more.
Row 5: K1, (P1, K1) twice, C6B, K1, (P1, K1) to end.
Row 6: K1, (P1, K1) twice, P6, K1, (P1, K1) to end.
Row 7: (K1, P1) twice, K8, (P1, K1) to end.
Row 8: K1, (P1, K1) twice, P6, K1, (P1, K1) to end.

Row 9: (K1, P1) twice, K8, (P1, K1) to end.
Row 10: K1, (P1, K1) twice, P6, K1, (P1, K1) to end.
Row 11: K1, (P1, K1) twice, C6B, K1, (P1, K1) to end.
Repeat rows 6–11 nine more times.
Next row: Work as row 2.
Next row: Work as row 1.
Next row: Knit. (This creates garter stitch ridge for turn over at top of pocket.)
Next row: Knit.
Next row: Purl.
Next row: Knit.
Next row: Purl.
Bind off.

Striped pocket

Cast on 11 sts using F and US 3 (3.25 mm) needles.

Row 1: (RS) Knit.

Row 2: (WS) Purl.

Change to G.

Row 3: Knit.

Row 4: Purl.

The last 4 rows form the stripe pattern. Repeat these 4 rows 15 more times, ending with a WS row.

Change to F.

Next row: Knit.

Next row: Knit. (This creates garter stitch ridge for turn over at top of pocket.)

Next row: Knit.

Next row: Purl.

Next row: Knit.

Next row: Purl.

Bind off.

Garter stitch pocket

Cast on 9 sts using H and US 8 (5 mm) needles.

Row 1: Knit.

This row forms the garter stitch pattern. Repeat row until pocket measures 8 in. (20 cm) from cast-on edge, ending with a RS row.

Next row: Knit. (This creates garter stitch ridge for turn over at top of pocket.)

Next row: Knit

Next row: Purl.

Next row: Knit.

Next row: Purl.

Bind off.

Fair Isle chart

☒	Yarn C
☐	Yarn E

Fair Isle pocket

Cast on 27 sts using E and US 3 (3.25 mm) needles.

Row 1: (RS) Knit.

Row 2: (WS) Purl.

Next, work rows 1–4 of Fair Isle chart. Repeat these 4 chart rows 14 more times, ending with chart row 4 (WS row).

Next row: Knit.

Next row: Knit. (This creates garter stitch ridge for turn over at top of pocket.)

Next row: Knit.

Next row: Purl.

Next row: Knit.

Next row: Purl.

Bind off.

Finishing

Lay the outer section on a flat surface with wrong side facing you. Place the inner section on top of the outer section with right side facing. Turn in the knitted hems of the outer section and sew in place. Fold the tops of the pockets at ridge row and sew on WS.

Position the first pocket approx. 2³/₄ in. (7 cm) in from the left-hand edge and 2¹/₂ in. (6 cm) up from the bottom and sew in place. In the same way position the last pocket approx. 2³/₄ in. (7 cm) in from the right-hand edge and 2¹/₂ in. (6 cm) up from the bottom and sew in place. Position and sew the remaining four pockets evenly in between.

Cut the ribbon in half. Lay the needle holder on a flat surface with the right side of the outer section facing you. Mark the points to secure the ribbon as follows: measure 5¹/₄ in. (13 cm) down from top right corner and place first marker and 5¹/₄ in. (13 cm) up from the bottom right corner and place a second marker. Measure 4 in. (10 cm) to the left of first marker and place a third marker and then 4 in. (10 cm) left of that and place a fourth marker. Starting at the second marker, place the fifth and sixth markers in the same way. You now have six points at which to secure the two lengths of ribbon. Allowing 18 in. (46 cm) excess of ribbon to hang free at the right-hand side of the holder, sew into place at the marked points. Do the same for the second length of ribbon.

reef

Keep your knitting organized and all your notions in one place with this cabled pencil case with a decorative pom-pom accent. A zipper closure ensures that you never mislay a stitch marker or cable needle again!

Materials
One 50g ball of Rowan Denim, Color 225 Nashville
US 6 (4mm) needles
Cable needle
Lining fabric, approx. 12 × 20 in. (30 × 50 cm)
One zipper, approx. 7$\frac{1}{4}$ in. (18 cm) long
Two circles of cardboard, approx. 1 in. (2.5 cm) in diameter
Sewing needle and thread

Gauge
Before washing:
20 sts and 28 rows to 4 in. (10 cm) measured over St st using US 6 (4 mm) needles.
After washing:
20 sts and 32 rows to 4 in. (10 cm) measured over St st using US 6 (4 mm) needles.

Finished size: 7$\frac{1}{4}$ × 5$\frac{1}{4}$ in. (18 × 13 cm)

Abbreviation
C4B Cable 4 Back: Slip next 2 sts onto cable needle and hold at back of work. Knit 2 sts from left needle and then knit the 2 sts from the cable needle.

C4F Cable 4 Front: Slip next 2 sts onto cable needle and hold at front of work. Knit 2 sts from left needle and then knit the 2 sts from the cable needle.

Front
Cast on 32 sts using US 6 (4 mm) needles.
Row 1: K3 (P1, K8) to last 2 sts, P1, K1.
Row 2: (K1, P1, K1, P6) to last 5 sts, K1, P1, K3.
Row 3: K3, P1, K3, C4F, (K1, P1, K3, C4F) to last 3 sts, K1, P1, K1.
Row 4: Work as row 2.
Row 5: K3, (P1, K1, C4B, K3) to last 2 sts, P1, K1.
Row 6: Work as row 2.
Repeat rows 3–6 until work measures 8$\frac{3}{4}$ in. (22 cm) from cast-on edge, ending with a WS row. Bind off in pattern.

Back
Cast on 25 sts using US 6 (4 mm) needles.
Row 1: Knit.
Row 2: K3, purl to end.
Repeat last 2 rows until work measures 8$\frac{3}{4}$ in. (22 cm) from cast-on edge, ending with a WS row.

Finishing
Rowan Denim shrinks in length when washed for the first time, so the front, back, and enough yarn to sew up and to make a pom-pom, must be washed following the instructions on the ball band, before the bag is sewn together.

With the garter stitch edge at the top, use mattress stitch to join the front and back by working down one side, across the bottom and up the other side.

Make fabric lining as follows:
Using the knitted pencil case as a template, cut two pieces of lining fabric slightly larger than the knitted pieces plus $\frac{3}{8}$ in. (1 cm) all around for the seam allowance. Sew a $\frac{3}{8}$ in. (1 cm) hem across the top edges of both pieces then sew them together along the other three sides. Turn the pencil case inside out, and with the lining fabric also inside out, sew the bottom two corners of the lining to the bottom two corners of the pencil case. Keeping the lining inside out, turn the pencil case back over it, so it is right side out with the lining inside. With the zipper open, trap the fabric edge of the zipper between the fabric lining and the knitted pencil case and sew into position.

Make pom-pom as follows:
Cut a hole in the center of each circle of cardboard approx. $\frac{5}{8}$ in. (1$\frac{1}{2}$ cm) in diameter. Wind the yarn throught the hole and around the outside of the two circles until the center hole is almost filled. Cut carefully round the edges of the cardboard until all the yarn has been cut. Ease the pieces of cardboard apart but before taking them off completely, tie a piece of yarn in a secure knot around the center of the pom-pom to hold it together. Remove the cardboard. Cut an approx. 5$\frac{1}{2}$ in. (14 cm) length of yarn and fold in half. Sew the two cut ends to the center of the pom-pom, to make a loop. Thread the loop through the zipper pull and folding the pom-pom back through it to secure.

minty

Your mobile phone or iPod will fit snugly inside this cute little cozy. A simple Fair Isle trim has been secured with a large button.

Materials

Yarn A One 50g ball of Rowan Cotton Glace, Color 809 Pier

Yarn B One 50g ball of Rowan Cotton Glace, Color 817 Maritime

US 4 (3.5 mm) needles

One turquoise button (Rowan 00369), 1 in. (2.5 cm) diameter

Gauge

23 sts and 32 rows to 4 in. (10 cm) on US 3 (3.25 mm) needles measured over stockinette stitch.

Finished·size: 3 × 4¾ in. (7.5 × 12 cm)

Front and Back (make one of each)

Cast on 18 sts using B and US 3 (3.25 mm) needles.

Row 1: (RS) Knit.

Row 2: (WS) Purl.

Repeat last 2 rows once more, ending with a WS row.

Row 5: Knit.

Row 6: Knit. (This creates garter st ridge for turn over at top.)

Change to A.

Row 7: Knit.

Row 8: Purl.

Repeat last 2 rows until work measures 5½ in. (14 cm) from cast-on edge, ending with a WS row.

Bind off.

Belt

Cast on 5 sts using B and US 3 (3.25 mm) needles.

Row 1: Knit.

Row 2: Purl.

Repeat last 2 rows 4 more times, ending with a WS row.

Next, work rows 1 and 2 of chart, below. Repeat these 2 chart rows until work measures 6¾ in. (17 cm) from cast-on edge, ending with a chart row 2.

Bind off using B.

Finishing

Turn under the top of the front section of the holder along the garter st ridge, and slip stitch into place using B. Do the same for the back.

Sew side seams.

Using the photograph as a guide, position the belt around the phone holder and where it overlaps with the section in B on top, sew the button into place neatly and securely.

X Yarn A

☐ Yarn B

petal

A colorful corsage adds a dash of feminity to anything, whether as a comely accent to a favorite outfit or an embellishment to other knitted pieces. Give this striking blossom extra dimension by using knitted leaves as a base.

Materials

Yarn A One 50g ball of Rowan Kidsilk Haze, Color 597 Jelly
Yarn B One 50g ball of Rowan Handknit Cotton, Color 314 Decadent
Yarn C One 50g ball of Rowan 4 ply Soft, Color 379 Goblin (used double)
US 6 (4 mm) needles
Safety pin

Gauge

22 sts and 30 rows to 4 in. (10 cm) using B on US 6 (4 mm) needles measured over stockinette stitch.

Finished size: Flower 2½ × 2½ in. (6 × 6 cm)
Including leaves 3½ × 3½ in. (9 × 9 cm)

Flower

Cast on 141 sts using A and US 6 (4 mm) needles. Change to B.
Row 1: (RS) K1, (K2, lift first of these sts over second) to end. (71 sts)
Row 2: (WS) P1, (P2tog) to end. (36 sts)
Row 3: K2, (K1, K2tog) to last 4sts, K4. (26 sts)
Row 4: Purl.
Break yarn and thread through remaining sts and pull together. Twist into flower shape and sew to secure.

Small leaf

Cast on 3 sts using C and US 6 (4 mm) needles.
Row 1: (WS) K1, P1, K1.
Row 2: (RS) K1, M1, K1, M1, K1. (5 sts)
Row 3: K1, P3, K1.
Row 4: K2, M1, K1, M1, K2. (7 sts)
Row 5: K1, P5, K1.
Row 6: Knit.
Row 7: K1, P5, K1.
Row 8: K2, sl 2, K1, p2sso, K2. (5 sts)
Row 9: K1, P3, K1.
Row 10: K1, sl 2, K1, p2sso, K1. (3 sts)
Row 11: K1, P1, K1.
Row 12: Sl 2, K1, p2sso. (1 st)
Fasten off. *

First large leaf

Cast on 3 sts using B and US 6 (4 mm) needles.
Row 1: (WS) K1, P1, K1.
Row 2: (RS) K1, M1, K1, M1, K1. (5 sts)
Row 3: K1, P3, K1.
Row 4: K2, M1, K1, M1, K2. (7 sts)
Row 5: K1, P5, K1.
Row 6: K3, M1, K1, M1, K3. (9 sts)
Row 7: K1, P7, K1.
Row 8: K4, M1, K1, M1, K4. (11 sts)
Row 9: K1, P9, K1.
Row 10: Knit.
Row 11: K1, P9, K1.
Row 12: K4, sl 2, K1, p2sso, K4. (9 sts)
Row 13: K1, P7, k1.
Row 14: K3, sl 2, K1, p2sso, K3. (7 sts)
Row 15: K1, P5, K1.
Row 16: K2, sl 2, K1, p2sso, K2. (5 sts)
Row 17: K1, P3, K1.
Row 18: K1, sl 2, K1, p2sso, K1. (3 sts)
Row 19: K1, P1, K1.
Row 20: Sl 2, K1, p2sso. (1 st)
Fasten off. *

> **note**
> When fastening off, leave enough yarn to sew along the length of the petal so that the end can be hidden in the center of the flower at the back.

Second large leaf

Work as for first large leaf, using C instead of B.

Finishing

Sew leaves to back of flower neatly and securely, using the photograph as a guide. Attach a safety pin to back of the corsage.

clematis

Five large petals form this larger-than-life floral brooch. With a cluster of decorative beads and long beaded tassels, this is a must for accessorizing!

Materials
Yarn A One 50g ball of Rowan Handknit Cotton, Color 313 Slick
Yarn B One 25g ball of Rowan Kidsilk Haze, Color 606 Candy Girl (used double)
US 3 (3.25 mm) needles
Approx. 10 large pink beads, 0.5 cm
Safety pin

Gauge
20 sts and 32 rows to 4 in. (10 cm) using A on US 3 (3.25 mm) needles measured over stockinette stitch.

Finished size: $4^3/_4 \times 4^3/_4$ in. (12 × 12 cm)

Large petal (make 5)
Cast on 3 sts using A.
Row 1: (WS) K1, P1, K1.
Row 2: (RS) K1, M1, K1, M1, K1. (5 sts)
Row 3: K1, P3, K1.
Row 4: K2, M1, K1, M1, K2. (7 sts)
Row 5: K1, P5, K1.
Row 6: K3, M1, K1, M1, K3. (9 sts)
Row 7: K1, P7, K1.
Row 8: K4, M1, K1, M1, K4. (11 sts)
Row 9: K1, P9, K1.
Row 10: Knit.
Row 11: K1, P9, K1.
Row 12: K4, sl 2, K1, p2sso, K4. (9 sts)
Row 13: K1, P7, K1.

Row 14: K3, sl 2, K1, p2sso, K3. (7 sts)
Row 15: K1, P5, K1.
Row 16: K2, sl 2, K1, p2sso, K2. (5 sts)
Row 17: K1, P3, K1.
Row 18: K1, sl 2, K1, p2sso, K1. (3 sts)
Row 19: K1, P1, K1.
Row 20: Sl 2, K1, p2sso. (1 st)
Fasten off. *

Small petal (make 5)
Cast on 3 sts using B.
Row 1: (WS) K1, P1, K1.
Row 2: (RS) K1, M1, K1, M1, K1. (5 sts)
Row 3: K1, P3, K1.
Row 4: K2, M1, K1, M1, K2. (7 sts)
Row 5: K1, P5, K1.
Row 6: Knit.
Row 7: K1, P5, K1.
Row 8: K2, sl 2, K1, p2sso, K2. (5 sts)
Row 9: K1, P3, K1.
Row 10: K1, sl 2, K1, p2sso, K1. (3 sts)
Row 11: K1, P1, K1.
Row 12: Sl 2, K1, p2sso. (1 st)
Fasten off. *

> ### note
> When fastening off, leave enough yarn to sew along the length of the petal so that the end can be hidden in the center of the flower at the back.

Finishing
Using the photograph as a guide, arrange the five large petals into a "star" shape and sew together in the middle to secure. Place the five smaller petals on top of the larger petals and secure in the same way. Sew five beads into the center of the flower.

Cut five pieces of yarn of varying lengths—approx. 6 in. (15 cm), $4^3/_4$ in. (12 cm), 4 in. (10 cm), $2^1/_2$ in. (6 cm) and $1^1/_2$ in. (4 cm)—and thread a bead onto the end of each one, then secure with a knot. Using the photograph as a guide, and allowing the beads to hang at the front of the flower, sew the five pieces of yarn into the flower center and secure at the back.

Attach a safety pin to back of the corsage.

zest

A wide Fair Isle band doubles as a stylish cuff, secured with a large button fastening. This design could be adapted in several ways, such as making it wider, narrower or using a different fastening.

Materials

Yarn A One 50g ball of Rowan Cotton Glace, Color 787 Hyacinth

Yarn B One 50g ball of Rowan Cotton Glace, Color 814 Shoot

US 3 (3.25 mm) needles

One purple button (Rowan 00374) 1 in. (2.5 cm) diameter

Lining fabric, approx. 3 1/4 in. × 7 1/4 in. (8 × 18 cm)

Sewing needle and thread

Gauge

23 sts and 32 rows to 4 in. (10 cm) on US 3 (3.25 mm) needles measured over stockinette stitch.

Finished size: 2 1/4 × 8 1/4 in. (5.5 × 20.5 cm)

Bracelet

Cast on 13 sts using A and US 3 (3.25 mm) needles.

Row 1: (RS) Knit.

Row 2: (WS) Purl.

Repeat last 2 rows once more, ending with a WS row.

Row 5: K5, bind off center 3 sts, Knit to end.

Row 6: P5, turn, cast on center 3 sts (see tip), turn, purl to end.

Row 7: Knit.

Row 8: Purl.

Begin working chart rows 1 and 2 (see below). Repeat these 2 chart rows until work measures 7 1/4 in. (18 cm) from cast-on edge, ending with chart row 2 (WS).

Continue in A only.

Next row: Knit.

Next row: Purl.

Repeat last 2 rows 3 more times, ending with a WS row.

Bind off.

Finishing

Sew button approx. 5/8 in. (1.5 cm) in from the bound-off edge.

Make fabric lining as follows:

Using the knitted bracelet as a template, cut out a piece of lining fabric slightly larger than the knitted piece plus 3/8 in. (1 cm) all around for the seam allowance. Sew a 3/8 in. (1 cm) hem all the way around all four edges, as they will be seen. Slip stitch the fabric to the back of the bracelet, covering all the fair Isle work and leaving the two ends unlined so button fastening can be used.

13 12 11 10 9 8 7 6 5 4 3 2 1

☐ Yarn A

☒ Yarn B

shimmer

This dazzling necklace is knitted from wire. The beads provide a glittering effect, and long beaded tassels are used as a simple fastening.

Materials
One spool of 28-gauge craft wire
Small amount of Rowan 4 ply Cotton,
   Color 129 Aegean
One pair US 3 (3.25 mm) double-pointed needles
Approx. 91 turquoise beads, 3 mm (J3001013) to
   fit on wire

Finished size: $^3/_8$ × 12$^1/_4$ in. (1 × 31 cm)
   (excluding ties)

Abbreviation
PB Place Bead: Bring wire forward between needles, slip bead to front of work, sl 1 purlwise, take wire to back of work. Bead will now be sitting in front of the slipped stitch. See "Knitting with beads" on page 80.

Necklace
The necklace is made using a technique sometimes known as either a "knitted cord" or an "I-cord". Once you have cast on your sts you knit one row. Do not turn. Instead, slide the sts to the other end of the double-pointed needle ready to be knitted again. The wire will now be at the left edge of the knitting and so to knit you must pull it tightly across the back of your work and then knit one row. Continue in this way, never turning and always sliding the work to the other end of the double pointed needle; the right side of the work will always be facing you.

Using the technique as described, make the necklace as follows:
Cast on 5 sts using US 3 (3.25 mm)
   double-pointed needles.
Row 1: (RS) Knit.
Repeat this row 7 more times.
Row 9: K1, PB, K1, PB, K1.
Row 10: Knit.
Row 11: K2, PB, K2.
Row 12: Knit.
Repeat last 4 rows until work
   measures 11 in. (28 cm)
   from cast-on edge, ending
   with row 9.
Next row: Knit.
Repeat last row seven more times.
Bind off.

Ties
Cut two 14 in. (35 cm) lengths of 4 ply Cotton. Fold one strand in half, then thread the folded loop through the center of the cast-on edge, fold the ends back through the loop and pull to secure. Do the same with the second strand at the center of the bound-off edge. Thread five beads onto the end of each of the strands of cotton, and secure with a knot.

emerald

This beaded wire bracelet has been knitted long enough to wrap around the wrist twice before fastening.

Materials
One spool of 28-gauge craft wire
One pair US 3 (3.25mm) double-pointed needles
Approx. 72 green beads (J3001022) to fit wire
Clasp

Finished size: 1/4 × 16 in. (0.5 × 40 cm)
   (excluding ties)

Abbreviation
PB Place Bead: Bring wire forward between needles, slip bead to front of work, sl 1 purlwise, take wire to back of work. Bead will now be sitting in front of the slipped stitch. See "Knitting with beads" on page 80.

Bracelet
The bracelet is made using a technique sometimes known as either a "knitted cord" or an "I-cord". Once you have cast on your sts you knit one row. Do not turn. Instead, slide the sts to the other end of the double pointed needle ready to be knitted again. The wire will now be at the left edge of the knitting, so to knit you must pull it tightly across the back of your work and then knit one row. Continue in this way, never turning and always sliding the work to the other end of the double pointed needle; the right side of the work will always be facing you.

Using the technique as described, make the bracelet as follows:
Cast on 3 sts using US 3 (3.25 mm) double-pointed needles.
Row 1: (RS) Knit.
Row 2: (RS) K1, PB, K1.
Repeat these last 2 rows until work measures 16 in. (40 cm) from cast-on edge.
Next row: Knit.
Bind off.

Finishing
Attach clasp to ends of bracelet using wire. Wear bracelet twisted twice around the wrist.

Knitting and Crochet Titles

America's Best-Loved Craft & Hobby Books®

CROCHET

Blankets, Hats, and Booties *NEW!*
Classic Crocheted Vests
Crochet from the Heart
Crochet for Babies and Toddlers
Crochet for Tots
Crocheted Aran Sweaters
Crocheted Lace
Crocheted Socks!
Crocheted Sweaters
Eye-Catching Crochet *NEW!*
The Essential Book of Crochet
    Techniques *NEW!*
First Crochet *NEW!*
Fun and Funky Crochet
The Little Box of Crocheted Hats
    and Scarves
The Little Box of Crocheted Ponchos
    and Wraps *NEW!*
More Crocheted Aran Sweaters
Today's Crochet

KNITTING

200 Knitted Blocks
365 Knitting Stitches a Year: Perpetual
    Calendar
Basically Brilliant Knits
Beyond Wool
Big Knitting *NEW!*
Blankets, Hats, and Booties *NEW!*
Classic Knitted Vests
Comforts of Home
Dazzling Knits
Everyday Style *NEW!*
Fair Isle Sweaters Simplified
First Knits
Funky Chunky Knitted Accessories *NEW!*
A Garden Stroll
Handknit Style
Knit It Now!
Knits for Children and Their Teddies
Knits from the Heart
Knitted Shawls, Stoles, and Scarves
Knitted Throws and More for the Simply
    Beautiful Home
The Knitter's Book of Finishing Techniques
A Knitter's Template

Knitting with Hand-Dyed Yarns
Knitting with Novelty Yarns
Knitter's Coasters *NEW!*
Lavish Lace
The Little Box of Knitted Ponchos and Wraps
The Little Box of Knitted Throws
The Little Box of Scarves
The Little Box of Scarves II
The Little Box of Sweaters
More Paintbox Knits
Perfectly Brilliant Knits
The Pleasures of Knitting
Pursenalities
Rainbow Knits for Kids
Ribbon Style *NEW!*
Sarah Dallas Knitting
Saturday Sweaters *NEW!*
Sensational Knitted Socks
Simply Beautiful Sweaters
Simply Beautiful Sweaters for Men
Style at Large
A Treasury of Rowan Knits
The Ultimate Knitted Tee
The Ultimate Knitter's Guide

Our books are available at bookstores and your favorite craft, fabric, and yarn retailers.
If you don't see the title you're looking for, visit us at www.martingale-pub.com or contact us at:
1-800-426-3126 • International: 1-425-483-3313 • Fax: 1-425-486-7596 • Email: info@martingale-pub.com